SPORT UNDER COMMUNISM

JAMES RIORDAN
editor

Sport under Communism

The U.S.S.R., Czechoslovakia,
The G.D.R., China, Cuba

McGILL–QUEEN'S UNIVERSITY PRESS
MONTREAL
1978

First published in the United Kingdom
by C. Hurst & Co. (Publishers) Ltd.,
1–2 Henrietta Street, London WC2E 8PS

Published simultaneously in Canada
by McGill–Queen's University Press,
1020 Pine Avenue West, Montreal H3A 1A2

© C. Hurst & Co. (Publishers) Ltd., 1978

ISBN 0–7735–0505–9

Legal deposit fourth quarter 1978
Bibliothèque Nationale du Québec

Printed in Great Britain

CONTENTS

v

PLATES

(between pages 86 and 87)

vii

PREFACE

In the space of a lifetime, the world has changed out of all recognition. As recently as 1930, a fifth of humanity resided within the British Empire—a political colouring which has now virtually disappeared from world atlases. In that same year, 1930, a single communist country existed, the USSR. Yet today, fifteen communist states on three continents encompass a third of the world population.

The pace of change is unrelenting, and its implications are worldwide. Whatever one may think of Communism as a way of life, the challenge it poses cannot be ignored in any sphere, be it politics, economics or, indeed, sport. Yet there is a regrettable dearth of serious knowledge and understanding of Communist countries, including their sports systems. Uninformed comment regularly takes the place of objective study and comparative assessment. Such attitudes do not aid our understanding of sport in Communist countries, nor help us to learn from them to enrich ourselves.

Worldwide interest in sport under Communism has grown principally in proportion to the success of Communist states in international sport, notably in the Olympic Games. The public imagination has been caught by such thrilling performers as Olga Korbut, Teofilo Stevenson, Kornelia Ender and Nadia Comeneci. Yet behind the stars and spectacles lie some revealing trends. First, when the Communist countries made their début at the Olympics in 1952, they won 29 per cent of the medals; in 1972 they won 47 per cent and in 1976 57 per cent. Secondly, at the 1976 Montreal Olympics, the German Democratic Republic, with a population of less than 17 million, won more gold medals than the USA, Canada, Britain and France combined; its women alone gained more medals than the rest of the world's women together. Thirdly, when it made its début in 1960, socialist Cuba came fifty-third of all the Olympic participants in the unofficial points total; by 1972 it had moved up to twenty-third; and in 1976 Cuba came eighth in the medal table. Fourthly, the USSR has "won" every Olympic Games, summer and winter, for which it has entered, with the sole exception of 1968, and is by far the most versatile nation in the history of the Olympics. In Montreal it won medals in nineteen of the twenty-one sports.

It is impossible to measure the impact of international sporting success on the behaviour of individuals and states. Nor would everyone agree that the health and strength of a society, least of all a Communist one, should be measured in terms of record-smashing or medal-winning. International sporting success nonetheless is visible and tangible testimony to the achievements of Communist sport. It is the aim of this book to look beyond these sporting victories at the sports systems that have made them possible. And it will be readily apparent that they have to be seen within the framework of new philosophies and concepts, notably of *physical culture*, that challenge the more traditional Western outlooks.

No pattern of recreation can be properly understood without reference to a country's physical and social environment. Therefore in no Communist state can sport be divorced from the state's climate and traditions, political and economic order or from military and international considerations. As the chapters in this book demonstrate, there is no *single* Communist system of sport, however similar many of the structural features may be.

It would perhaps have been best to invite native specialists to write on their own countries. That was my original intention; I do not hold that we in the West know best. If a dialogue is to be at all meaningful, it is essential that we listen to each other's viewpoints. However, such are the vagaries of international politics and distrust that I received a dusty response from Berlin, sympathetic but apologetic replies from Belgrade and Warsaw, an enthusiastic but tardy reception in Havana, and no response at all from Moscow and Peking. All the more credit therefore to Dr. Kostka of Czechoslovakia for his contribution.

It is no disrespect to the missing native contributors to suggest that the book is of more immediate value to the Western reader by combining the varied talents and critical faculties of two Canadians, a Czechoslovak and four Englishmen, straddling the diverse disciplines of physical education, political science and sociology. Each contributor has first-hand knowledge of his subject, having either lived in or made sports tours of the country concerned. Their chapters are placed in the chronological order of change to the new political order. The book is rightfully introduced by Don Anthony, a pioneer in the West of serious study of comparative sport, with a special interest in the developing countries of Eastern Europe and the Third World.

It is our hope that this joint endeavour will help to promote further understanding and toleration in sport, as in all human relationships.

Bradford   JAMES RIORDAN

Don Anthony

INTRODUCTION

Dr. Anthony lectures on comparative aspects of sport and physical education at Avery Hill College, England; he is a pioneer in Britain of the study of comparative sport, particularly in modernising societies in Eastern Europe and the Third World, having written his doctorate on "Comparative Physical Education" (Univ. of Leicester). For several years he was a consultant to UNESCO and the Council of Europe, adviser to the IAAF and several commercial companies on sport. More recently, he was co-founder of the Centre for International Sports Studies and initiator of the British International Festival of Sports Film and Television (Videosport). A former British Olympic hammer-thrower, he is a well-known sportswriter and commentator, having worked for the BBC at both the Mexico and Montreal Olympics. Among his publications are *Know the Game; Keeping Fit for all Ages; Volleyball—Do it this way*; and *The Dunlop P.E. Teacher's Handbook*. He is married to a graduate of the Warsaw Academy of Physical Culture and has one son, Marek.

One can compare similarities—or one can compare differences. I prefer the latter. The contents of this book highlight a great number of differences between the way we conceive of, and organise, the modern phenomenon of sport and physical education—and the manner in which five "socialist" countries conceive of, and organise, theirs. This is not a semantic exercise regarding the definition of socialism; I know there will be some who claim that real socialism has yet to be expressed in any nation-state. The five countries selected for study display important differences, one with another, as well as between them and us. Let us agree that they have all taken a "socialist way" in their approach to sport—and let us try to analyse the facts the authors present to us.

It is not necessary to approve of all they have done, and are doing, in sport and physical education. Not all is golden in the socialist sports camp—as even the committed socialists will tell you. They have much to learn from us. They also have much to teach. It is this two-way dialogue which makes the comparative study of problems so enriching. Too much of the comment and reportage concerning sports developments in the socialist countries has been unsympathetic and prejudiced. In recent years, however, even the most jaundiced Western reporters have paid grudging tribute to the development of certain aspects of sport in the socialist world. And, let us remember, this socialist world is enormous—involving, in terms of population, a third of mankind.

In my experience the socialist countries have always made a careful study of *our* experience. There is, for example, admiration of our "running culture" as the basis for success in athletics. There is, of course, the inbuilt advantage we have in our national language: not only are the rules of most sports framed in the English language, but even the descriptive "foul", "offside", "corner", and so on, have permeated in their original form most other languages. They also recognise that we "invented" most modern competitive sports and games—and that we exported them. Soccer to the Soviet Union; rowing to Germany. They recognise that we were always generous in our reception of sporting ambassadors from overseas, such as Mme. Osterberg from Sweden and Dr. Roth from Hungary, who made such significant contributions to the development of British physical education at the turn of this century.

It was also generally recognised that the English Public Schools introduced the idea that games could be an invaluable means of character training. Coubertin himself was strongly influenced by this concept as he formulated the principles of the modern Olympic movement. The British point of view about world sporting matters is still valued and it is extremely important that we try to maintain our reputation for fair play—not only on the playing fields, but also in the forums where people think about sport and physical education.

It was at the English Public Schools that games became a daily routine. The curriculum was so ordered that academic work took place in the mornings—sport in the afternoons. The socialist countries have tried, in a way, to structure the general schools pattern in that manner. The experience of Millfield is another case in point; a small group of privileged and talented children are encouraged to achieve real excellence in sports. The "socialists" try to extend that facility to a much wider spectrum of society.

Recently a leading British sportswriter wrote thus of the Oxford–Cambridge Boat Race:

At the moment the flag drops 16 oars will be pulled, surely, by the fittest sportsmen over the length of our land. Not necessarily the best, mark you, but the fittest. Since last year's leaves were still lush-green every one of them (plus a sad clutch who narrowly failed to make the boat) has been putting in a six hour day of intense physical discipline; sculling, distance running, rowing, sprinting, lifting weights high, shunning lights low; no wine, no women, daft songs. No Smoking By Order. Rowing and more rowing. Rhythm of Blues through sleet and snow, sodden sludge on their shorts . . . November, December, January, February. Living in each other's pockets. Living with each other's habits, like monks.[1]

And so it has been for the Oxbridge élites for more than 100 years. The modern training camp was another British invention; the idea of concentrated sports training for a few privileged amateurs—provided they were gentlemen—was a British concept. It was only when this invention and this concept were extended to the broad masses that hands were raised in horror and the cry of "professionalism" rent the air. It was only when the butchers and bakers, the clerks and bricklayers, the plumbers and engineers—especially those of Eastern Europe—applied the Oxbridge formula to sport, that the Cardinals of international sport protested.

It has been, and still is, difficult for those who lead sports in Western countries to understand the challenge thrown up by the socialist revolutions since 1917. The particular forms of sports democratisation which have evolved in Eastern Europe, in China, and in Cuba, often rock and shock those who hold to "bourgeois" principles. When a country decides that sport is a right and not a privilege—that sport is equal in status to science and art, that sport shall no longer be the preserve of the universities and colleges—there must be massive government intervention at both local and national level to make an idea into an actuality. When there is such government intervention, such investment of the public budget, there must be public accountability. If this means "bringing politics into sport", so be it. The interesting fact is, however, that most of the countries now classified as socialist have always seen sport as "politicised". When one studies the chapters in this book, one sees clearly that in Germany, in Czechoslovakia and in Russia the pre-socialist sporting associations reflected the political structures. There were "proletarian sports groups" and "monarchist sports groups"; the trade unions often saw sport as a means of reaching the millions.

If one looks at the development of world sport entirely through British spectacles it is, indeed, difficult to comprehend what has happened and what is happening. What happened in these islands one hundred years ago and more has little practical relevance to the developing world of today. The uniqueness of our own historical experience is not for general export. In the countries of the Third World struggling to build sports movements in an economy of scarcity, there are no leisure classes able and willing to organise sports as a hobby. Our own models are often clearly inappropriate, while the models of the socialist world are often particularly apt.

One of the most blatant errors made by those studying the socialist countries is to assume that they represent an amorphous "bloc". Although there are many common factors and shared principles, there are also big differences between, for example, Poland and Czechoslovakia, between Hungary and Bulgaria, and between them all and the USSR. In this book we have five different countries. The USSR—utilising sport as a means of changing society; integrating sport into a gigantic effort to take a backward and poor country of vast size from near-feudalism to modernity in sixty years. Czechoslovakia—inheriting a rich tradition in sports and physical education since the late nineteenth century; a country with three or four generations of industrialisation behind it. The German Democratic Republic—born of a divided and beaten Reich; reared in the heat of the Cold War; adapting the scientific systematisation of pre-war Germany to a Marxist–Leninist philosophy. Cuba, like the GDR—using sport as a means to break a cultural boycott; transforming sport from a highly professionalised entertainment into a means of public health and education. And China —inheritor of the oldest-known written form of physical training, proud possessor of a rich and ancient culture, employing sport as a means of social engineering and ethical education. The modern Chinese slogan—"Friendship First, Competition Second"—is perhaps the most powerful new idea to penetrate the world of sport in the last fifty years.

Dr. Riordan has assembled evidence from these five countries for analysis. He asked the authors to note five areas—history and development; the emergence of new features since their political watershed; the organisation and structure of contemporary sport; the organisation of physical education in schools; and the main goals of sport and physical education.

You will see that there are wide differences in the ways the authors have tackled their brief. It seems strange that we have waited so long for a book of this kind. Only one contributor, from Czechoslovakia, writes as a national working in sport and physical education in his own country. The German Democratic Republic chapter is written by a university lecturer who has researched assiduously and mixed this with personal experience and opinion. The section of China is written by two respected North American academics who have visited China several times. That on Cuba is written from the viewpoint of a leading sports commentator, well versed in sports organisation in more than sixty countries. Dr. Riordan's chapter on the USSR is illustrative of the enormous contribution he is making in the field of comparative studies. Before James Riordan took off for his five years' study and work in Moscow, we lacked a linguist and a scholar with personal knowledge of the USSR. Our references were culled from descriptive articles and propaganda news-sheets. Dr. Riordan brought to us the spirit of true scholarly enquiry and an analytical mind. There are not many Britons with his flair for languages, his love of sport, and his academic background. There are even fewer who can claim membership of a top Moscow sports club and ongoing domestic links with the USSR. All this then is the feast he set before us; allow me to comment more strictly on the five chapters.

The USSR, since it was, in a sense, first in the field, has always held a special charisma for us in the West. Lenin insisted as early as 1917 that a High School for Sports and Physical Culture should be built. He was convinced of the importance of sport in creating the harmonious "communist man" and his faith was never shaken. The Russian revolutionaries were also quick to understand the new rôle for trade unions in the sporting movement. Sport was an attractive means of rallying the masses to meetings. More modern thinking on the relationship between trade unions and sport shows that a higher quality of life can be secured by struggling for richer experience—as well as heavier wage packets.

It was the Soviet Union which introduced the policy of linking sport directly with a public health policy, a policy of organising sports opportunities for the very young, the talented and the aged. It was the Soviet Union which introduced the idea that stadiums should be owned—as well as built—by the community. It was its decision too that multi-sport clubs, with the rich and popular sections like soccer supporting the "minor" sports, were ideal for the Soviet development plans. Despite the preoccupation of the USSR with success at international level and the development of special sports training schools, there has been a concurrent drive to make "Sport for All" more than an empty clarion call. Despite the early antagonism of the International Olympic Committee (Dr. Riordan points out that the IOC recognised three Tsarist representatives between 1917 and 1932), later presidents of the IOC, including Avery Brundage and Lord Killanin, have testified to the successes of the USSR in sports and in achieving sport for all, and to the spirit of Olympism which permeates much of its sporting effort.

The traditional Czech "Sokol" movement was always highly politicised: its founders, Tyrs and Fugner, were passionate and militant nationalists who saw the sports and gymnastics movements as a form of para-military training. Their demand "Every Czech a Sokol"[2] was a symbolic cry for freedom for the Slavs. The Sokol movement was "mass" in theory and in fact. It involved millions of participants in simple gymnastic routines in the early stages – and tens of thousands in the final performances. The famous Strahov Stadium in Prague was designed not only for these thousands of participants but also for more than two hundred thousand spectators. The great Sokol Festivals were, in fact, the organisation model for the USSR Spartakiads. During the last thirty years the Czechs have been prominent in sports research and in sports medicine; they have organised a national network of "fitness screening" and sports injury treatment clinics. They have made distinct contributions to the study of sports history. In physical education their training of specialists has continued to be sophisticated, and their "refresher courses" every five years for physical education teachers—a lesson for us all. I think it would be true to say that in Czechoslovakia one can study the front-line experience of a country where some traditional Western sports concepts have met Marxist–Socialist principles head on.

The Germans of the East also came under the influence of Soviet thinking after the last war. The birth of the Democratic Republic was not easy; nor was its development. The GDR was cast out from the family of European nations and its athletes were refused visas to the most respected countries. And yet, in the end, the world sat up and took notice. Not only has the GDR "made the grade" economically, but its fame rides high in the world of sport. Indeed, it is today the most powerful nation in world competitive sports; it takes the lead in training sports leaders from the Third World and the leading European sports institute is at Leipzig. All this is not done at the expense of sport for all: health and fitness rooms exist in blocks of flats and on housing estates, and fitness testing facilities for everyone are provided in public parks. There is also innovation and invention: the sports boarding schools were a GDR innovation. Moreover, the GDR sports equipment industry is much respected throughout the world. The Germans, of course, inherit a long tradition in sport as well as in respect for science and the capacity for discipline and hard work.

Anyone who has heard Latin Americans greet Cuban teams with the cry "*Cuba si*" will realise the connection of sports success with cultural identity. All Latin Americans are immensely proud of Cuba's success. At last here is an area of human endeavour, they seem to think, where we can take on the North Americans and hold our own. Fidel Castro has taken sport and made it central to the revolution—in common with health, and culture and education. Prior to the revolution, he says, the stadiums were largely empty; we had some professional boxers and some professional baseball players. Now the stadiums are full, with a limited range of sports being played at a very high level. After several years of coaching-help from East European coaches, the Cuban coaching personnel are maintaining, and even enhancing, standards. The Cubans appear to have married their background of American "know-how" to socialist planning, and have not stifled the Latin exuberance which makes them such exciting and attractive athletes. The Cubans see the facilities, the equipment, and the teachers of sports and physical education, as belonging to the whole community—not merely to the schools or the clubs.

China is still a mystery to most of us. I met their volleyball teams at the 1956 World Championships in Paris. Thereafter—a long silence. A retreat into social development and cultural revolution. Some international federations cut them off from contact with the outside world, others ensured regular and sympathetic aid. Sometimes Albanian sports federations would arrange visits from Western sports leaders to "coincide" with those of the Chinese. Apart from the continuing participation in table tennis, highlighted by the "ping-pong" rapprochement with the USA, the Chinese drifted from the mainstream of world sport. In 1974, they signalled their intended return at the Asian Games in Teheran. Their large team at the Seventh Asian Games showed that there was much to be done but that the potential was there. There is no doubt that the Chinese will, when they so decide, achieve excellent levels in all sports. It could be, however, that "Friendship First, Competition Second" might really take root—and thus point to new pastures for all of us in sport.

Finally, I want to take an overall look at these five countries. The Slav countries possess one distinct advantage—in terminology. "Physical Culture" is an excellent description of all that we try to do in sport and physical education teaching. It is better than P.T., P.E., Movement, etc. It has helped the socialist countries to avoid the interminable terminological disputes that have racked the Anglo-Saxon and the French physical education professions these past twenty years. It has helped them avoid the "either-or" reasoning which has separated sport from physical education in some countries. In Physical Culture, championship sport and sport-for-all are seen as twin pillars of the same movement; as equal parts of the same sports spectrum. The GDR illustrates a feature which is common in many of the socialist countries—the youthfulness of the sports hierarchy. In countries where socialist governments took power after violent revolution the "old guard" in sports administration had either fled, was antagonistic, or was moved out of office. This youth factor has helped these countries to accept modern planning techniques in sports, to avoid tripping over the "amateur-professional" body at every step, to accept totally new ideas in sport. The social structure of society in the countries concerned has meant that "professionalism" has no validity; where the state is the ultimate employer "broken-time" payments are no problem. Here the full-time professional in the Western sense is meaningless. The structure of society has meant that it is easy for a sports "star" to be re-integrated into normal working life after his active sports days are over. It has also meant that "stars" can be fully utilised in the sports movement after retirement as teachers, coaches, leaders, organisers, etc. Interesting methods of honouring sports stars have been developed. There have been noteworthy attempts to create a variety of job opportunities in sports; the enthusiast is not restricted to the physical education teaching profession. The "sports for women" crusade has received an enormous boost from these countries. In the last five years there have been some astonishing compromises over principles. The rôle of the socialist nationals in world tennis is a case in point, with the national federations earning valuable foreign currency through the efforts of the individual players.

Sports futurology think-tanks have been quietly active in the socialist countries; here again GDR research is particularly interesting. There is some fascinating prediction of where sport might be going in the next fifty or one hundred years. The Polish experience, although not part of this book, is also worthy of mention. Polish links with the motherland have a particular significance for sports lovers. Most overseas groups of Poles support a "Polish Olympic Club"; this Club sponsors one or more athletes for the Olympic Games, money is raised, leading Polish athletes travel to speak at dinners and dances.

The whole operation is an example of cultural links triumphing over political differences.

The socialist countries have long been conspicuously absent from the committees of international sports federations. Most headquarters of international sports federations have long been in London or Switzerland. Recent years, however, have seen the glimmers of a new movement: the secretariat of international weightlifting has moved from London to Budapest; of boxing from London to Moscow. The British General Secretary of world basketball (FIBA) was replaced by a Yugoslav. Wrestling is presided over by another Yugoslav. This could be the beginning of a bigger transfer of power. For many years we introduced the world to such virtues as fair play and sportsmanship. It was easy, after all, when *we* did all the winning and *they* did all the losing! We have now had to come to terms with a transfer of power on the sporting battlefronts. It will be interesting to see how we can adapt as the administrative transfer also gather momentum. A further indication of this momentum is the mounting interest shown by the socialist countries in UNESCO. The call at the 1976 Nairobi General Conference of UNESCO for an Inter-Governmental Committee on Sports received a warm welcome from the socialist countries.

We are witnessing today the results of thirty years of sports planning in most of the socialist countries—sixty in the case of the USSR, and fifteen in the case of Cuba. We will soon have evidence to help us decide whether children who are "creamed off" for special sports training suffer any physical or mental harm, whether those who are selected early make the national teams regularly, and whether late developers appear in equal numbers. We might also pay attention to the fact that, despite a passion for "systematic planning", there are some remarkably flexible ways of training to be a teacher or a coach—with correspondence and vacation opportunities for the part-time student very much in evidence.

I hope, then, that this book will help to usher in a new era in world sport—an ongoing debate about goals, organisation, relationships between sport and government. I hope that it contributes to promoting a powerful dialogue between sports thinkers, sportswriters, physical education specialists, sports enthusiasts of all kinds.

This book appears prior to the 1980 Olympic Games, the first Olympics to be staged in a socialist country. There are many who claim that the Games are doomed, that they are too big, too costly, too nationalistic. However, the Moscow Games will, by and large, take place in a stadium and use facilities which already exist; this fact alone is a new development. It might be that the Moscow Games will focus attention on many more critical points in the Olympic structure, will suggest new ways of handling old problems. Certainly the most important aim for which all of us in sport must work—is to preserve the unity of world sport. A split down the middle would be disastrous for sport. It is not surprising that sport is beset by problems; in terms of history it is a youthful phenomenon. In 100 years international sport has grown from almost an eccentricity to a powerful social force involving hundreds of millions of people. It is astonishing that still today policies at the highest level are made by committees that meet irregularly, are understaffed for the gigantic tasks which confront them, and are badly served by institutional back-up expertise. Such books as this might help to redress the balance, might help those who are involved in decision-making more fully to comprehend the problems they face. This book might also nourish the general reader—the sports fan. It will help people to understand that sport is not something divorced from life but that it is, for millions, something more real and rewarding as an experience than those activities which are commonly accepted as real. It is, after all, in sport and physical activity that man often feels more totally expressive as a human being than in the activities of his normal working day.

NOTES

1. Frank Keating, *The Guardian*, 19 March, 1977, p. 5.
2. *Sokol* is the Czech word for "falcon".

James Riordan

THE U.S.S.R.

PERSONAL NOTE

Dr. Riordan is lecturer in Russian Studies at Bradford University, England. For five years he lived, studied and worked in the USSR, playing regularly for the Moscow *Spartak* badminton team and making special sports tours of the Baltic republics, Central Asia and the Caucasus. On his return he wrote a doctoral dissertation on the development of Soviet sport and physical education (University of Birmingham, 1975) and a book *Sport in Soviet Society* (Cambridge University Press, 1977). His other publications include *Sport and Physical Education in the Soviet Union: an Outline*, and several collections of folk tales. He is married to a Soviet Tartar ex-schoolteacher.

CONTENTS

Introduction

Among the reasons for studying Soviet sport the following would seem to be most cogent and revealing.

First, the USSR is the most successful nation in the history of international sports competition. Not only has it "won" every Olympic Games, summer and winter, for which it has entered (with the sole exception of 1968) it is by far the most versatile nation in Olympic history, participating in every Olympic event except field hockey. A sports system that can consistently achieve such success certainly merits attention for what it can teach others in areas of sporting proficiency, including its awards and rankings programme, coaching, professional training, sports schools, clubs and sports boarding schools.

Second, sporting excellence in the USSR is largely complementary to sport for all. Soviet athletes are successful not because they constitute a privileged élite, but because the society they live in makes the widest possible provision for all to take part in sport. Social pressure excites the motivation which, added to a government-aided base, a national fitness programme for virtually all age groups and free access to the means of pursuing sport, is said to involve nearly a quarter of the population in regular and active sport.

Third, not only has the Soviet Union a different sports system to Western states, its entire sporting philosophy is radically at variance with our own. It echoes the Marxist notion of the interdependence of the physical and mental states of human beings, so that physical culture is treated equally with mental culture in a person's upbringing—both for the all-round development of the individual and, ultimately, for the health of society. Moreover, in Soviet development, sport has been accorded the vital rôle of *helping to change society*. It has to be remembered that the USSR is a modernising as well as a socialist society, with all the problems of a population in transition from the country to the town, from a traditional folk culture to an urban industrial way of life, from abject poverty to relative prosperity; this has been achieved at enormous sacrifice and almost wholly on its own resources.

Fourth, Soviet influence in sport on the rest of the world is far-reaching, more so than most countries care to admit. During the inter-war period, the Chinese borrowed heavily; in the immediate postwar period, the Soviet sports structure, shaped by peculiar Soviet conditions, was largely imposed upon or hastily copied by all Eastern European states; in the last two decades extensive assistance in sport has been extended to other socialist nations and many developing countries of Africa, Asia and Latin America—this is likely to accelerate in the future. Soviet impact on the West is also substantial, as illustrated by the choosing of Moscow as the venue for the 1980 Olympics, increasing exchanges and studies, the adopting of Soviet experience in many countries, from France to Australia, and the growing re-examination of domestic sports policies and even the future of international sports bodies.

We shall in the course of this chapter try to adumbrate the salient formative influences on Soviet sport and physical education, to outline the main course of their development and to examine the rôle of sport in Soviet society.

I. *Historical development*

The Russian Revolution of October 1917 brought a rupture with the past in many ways, yet several aspects of Soviet sport, as of other areas of social life, still show, if not continuity with the past, at least strong influence by factors having their origins outside the Soviet period. It would certainly be wrong to imagine that a totally new structure, inspired only by new ideas, was created after 1917. The roots of Soviet sport in part lie deep in Russian history, in the people's habits and traditions, the climate, the state's preoccupation with external and internal foes, the intellectual ferment of Russian society in the latter part of the nineteenth and early twentieth centuries. It would have been strange, indeed, if these currents played much less a rôle in shaping the practice of sport in the Soviet Union than the social thought of foreign philosophers—and these, it must be realised, included Rousseau as well as Marx. In addition, foreign practice, in the form of organised sports pioneered for urban industrial society largely by Britain, the gymnastics schools of Germany, the Scandinavian countries and the Czech lands, and Prussian military training all put their imprint on Soviet sport and physical education.

The amalgam of ideas and institutions, rather eclectically selected for application in Soviet policy-making, was to depend on short- and middle-term expediency as well as ideology, as variously interpreted at different stages of Soviet history.

(i) *Militarisation of sport 1917–20*

When the Bolsheviks seized power, they found a country on the verge of economic collapse. Civil war and foreign intervention accelerated and intensified radical transformations in the economy and politics. The Bolsheviks were at war, and centralised control in the interests of war-production was an obvious recourse. *The impact of this initial period on the whole of Soviet history is very great:*

It cannot be emphasised too much that . . . the regime was emerging from the civil war and had been shaped by that war as much as by the doctrines of the Party.[1]

It was against the background, then, of war and cataclysmic events that the new, universal system of physical education and sport that Bolshevik educationalists had been advocating before the Revolution had to be introduced. The first steps to be taken were by no means obvious, for there was no pattern to follow; the change-over from criticism of capitalist institutions and the sports structure of industrial states to practical action in an eighty per cent peasant society in the throes of civil war, however, presented immense problems. What of the past was valid and useful? What had to be discarded? Was the bourgeois legacy (of organised sports, leagues and cups, clubs and gymnastics systems) a cancer that had to be cut out of the Russian body to make it healthy or could the best of bourgeois practice be adapted to serve the needs of the struggling proletarian state? Was there any social value in attempts to break records? These were the types of questions that were being debated, often furiously, in educational circles during this initial period.

The first few years were, naturally, a period of improvisation and experiment, with several groups eager to implement their theories The regime was to take some measures that were later to be revoked or regretted, but which, at the time, were mainly dictated by the chaos and uncertainty and the "besieged military camp" atmosphere. Essentially, however, sport during the period known as War Communism came to be geared to the needs of the war-effort. On 7 May 1918, by a decree of the All-Russia Central Executive Committee of the Soviets of Workers', Soldiers' and Peasants' Deputies, a new government agency was set up: the Central Board of Universal Military Training—*Vsevobuch*. Its main aim was

to supply the Red Army with contingents of trained conscripts as quickly as possible.[2]

One means of achieving this was to carry out a crash programme of physical fitness; accordingly, *Vsevobuch* was given control of all sports clubs and societies and made responsible for the physical training of all people of recruitable (18–40) and pre-recruitment (16–18) age.

In line with the policy of combining military drill and weapon-handling with political and general education in elementary hygiene, it was also decided to coordinate the activities of *Vsevobuch* with those of the Commissariats of Education and Health. In the opinion of Nikolai Podvoisky, the head of *Vsevobuch*, it was impossible to bring the Civil War to a successful conclusion or to build socialism without a large-scale campaign to improve physical fitness and health.

A second major consideration, then, was health. Having inherited a country with an inclement climate, whose population was over-whelmingly illiterate, where disease and starvation were common and where most people had only a rudimentary knowledge of hygiene, the Soviet leaders appreciated that it would take a radical economic and social transformation to alter the situation substantially. But time was short, and able-bodied and disciplined men were vital, first for the country's survival, then for its recovery from the ravages of war and revolution, for industrial development and defence against further probable-seeming attacks.

Regular participation in physical exercise was to be one—relatively inexpensive but effective—means of improving health standards rapidly and a channel by which to educate people in hygiene, nutrition and exercise. One indication of the health policy being pursued was the campaign during the Civil War under the slogans "Help the Country with a Tooth-Brush!", "Help the Country by Observing the Dry (i.e. Prohibition) Law!" and "Physical Culture Twenty-Four Hours a Day!" With the influx of masses of peasants into the cities (bringing with them rural habits), the significance of health through physical exercise took on a new dimension.

The ignorance which was the cause of so much disease, starvation and misery—and which hampered both military effectiveness and labour-productivity—was to be combated by a far-reaching programme of physical exercise and sport. And if the material facilities were lacking, then people were urged to make full use of

the sun, air, water and natural movement—the best proletarian doctors.[8]

The campaign could only catch on, in Podvoisky's opinion, if the emotional attraction of *competitive* sport were to be utilised to the utmost—this at a time when "competition" and "sport" had become rather "dirty" words; certainly, a number of educationalists regarded competitive sport as debasing physical culture and inculcating non-socialist habits. This was a view held, for example, by the Education Commissar Lunacharsky; it had been subscribed to previously by the pre-revolutionary physical educationalist Pyotr Lesgaft. Nonetheless, competitive sport and contests began to be organised from the lowest level upwards, culminating in the All-Russia Pre-Olympiads and the First Central Asian Olympics of 1920. The pre-Olympiads were to set the stage for a national festival of physical culture timed to coincide with the Second Congress of the Third International in 1920. In honour of this event, some 18,000 people participated in a huge gymnastics and sports display in the new Red Stadium in Moscow. The Tashkent games, which were given the prestigious title of the First Central Asian Olympics, lasted for ten days in early October 1920. As many as 3,000 people took part, mostly natives of Turkestan. The significance of this sports festival in Turkestan for the Soviet national policy of the time may be judged by the fact that this was the first time that Uzbeks, Kazakhs, Turkmenians, Kirgiz and other local peoples, as well as Russians, had competed in any sporting event together.[4] As was made clear later, the authorities regarded sport as an important means of integrating the diverse peoples of the old Russian Empire in the new Soviet state:

The integrative functions of sport are great. This has immense importance for our multinational state. Sports contests, festivals, spartakiads and other types of sporting competition have played an important part in cementing the friendship of Soviet peoples.[5]

Integrative policies aside, these sporting initiatives should be seen as a highly principled aspect of the general cultural emancipation of what were formerly subject peoples.

Thus, already at the dawn of the Soviet state, three principal ingredients of the sports policy—for *health, defence* and *integration*—were made explicit by the new regime.

In principle, the fate of the Civil War and foreign intervention was settled in November 1920. The new state was now to enter a period of restoration and reconstruction. The end of the period of hostilities also signified the demise of *Vsevobuch*, since it had served its purpose. The military organisation of sport was no longer necessary in peacetime, and new methods had to be found which would be more in tune with the new social conditions.

(ii) *Years of physical culture 1921–9*

This was a decisive period for the future of Soviet society, with the death of Lenin and the acute struggle in many spheres of life. By the end of this "experimental" period, known as that of the New Economic Policy, Stalin's pre-eminence was unchallenged and the whole country was launched into an all-out campaign to industrialise and modernise.

Just as in other fields of endeavour, in sport this was a time of constant discussion. Controversy raged over its rôle in a workers' state and its organisational structure, with various groups contending for influence. Basically, however, these were the years of *physical culture* rather than sport, the dividing-line between the two being the presence of an element of competition. Competitive sport bred in some people's minds attitudes alien to socialist society.

The strongest proponents of physical culture and keenest critics of *Vsevobuch* (for its alleged "sportisation" and "militarisation" of physical culture) were known as the hygienists. They were mainly medical people: physiologists, anatomists, health workers who were concerned about the need to improve health standards. One means they saw to make people aware of personal hygiene and bodily fitness was physical culture—which many of them contrasted sharply with "sport". Such pursuits as weightlifting, boxing and gymnastics were, in their opinion, irrational and dangerous, encouraged individualist rather than collectivist attitudes and values—and, as such, were contrary to the desired socialist ethic. One result of pressure from the hygienists was the reduction of the number of contests that took place in the 1920s and the exclusion from those contests that did take place of certain "harmful" sports. The First Trade Union Games, in 1925, for example, excluded soccer, boxing, weightlifting and gymnastics from its programme, even though these were four of the most popular (in terms of participation) sporting pursuits in the country at the time. Boxing was outlawed in the same year in the Leningrad Region by order of the Leningrad Physical Culture Council.

A second influential group in the 1920s was the Proletkultists,[6] who demanded the rejection of competitive sport and all organised sports that derived from bourgeois society, as remnants of the decadent past and emanations of degenerate bourgeois culture. A fresh start had to be made through the "revolutionary innovation of proletarian physical culture", which would take the form of "labour gymnastics" and mass displays, pageants and excursions. Gymnasiums and their "bourgeois" equipment would be replaced by various pieces of apparatus on which young proletarians could practise their "labour movements".

The Proletkultists, therefore, went much further than the hygienists in condemning all kinds of games, sports and gymnastics "tainted" by bourgeois society. In a book called *New Games for New Children* which they had published, the Proletkultists advocated such new games as "Swelling the Ranks of Children's Communist Groups", "Rescue from the Fascists", "Agitators", "Helping the Proletarians", and "Smuggling Revolutionary Literature across the Frontier".[7]

Subsequently, several Proletkultist notions were taken up and incorporated in Soviet sport, while their originators were rejected (and mostly liquidated after 1934). "Production gymnastics" (physical exercises at work) were, for example, to be taken up on a mass scale with the onset of the First Five-Year Plan in 1928 and are today a distinctive feature of Soviet physical culture—though their purpose is more utilitarian than aesthetic, more geared to higher productivity than the proletarian bodily perfection that the Proletkultists advocated. Further-more, the attempted portrayal of proletarian grandeur and the Soviet messianic mission in sporting displays, pageants, children's games and even art forms, so favoured by the Proletkultists, is as strong today as it ever was.

Concerned at the continuing bickering and ambiguity in organisation and roles of sport, the Party issued its first authoritative statement on sport in a historic document of 13 July 1925, entitled "On the Tasks of the Party in Physical Culture".[8] In essence, the Party declared that sport was to be a means for achieving (a) better health and physical fitness; (b) character-formation, as part of general education in pro-ducing a harmonious personality; (c) military training; and (d) the identification of individuals with groups (Party, Soviet, trade-union) and their encouragement to be active socially and politically. In rejecting the principal views of both the hygienists and the Proletkultists, the Party made it clear that, properly controlled by medical and educational personnel, competitive activities could be valuable in drawing more people into sport; it could also be used to raise levels of skill. Sporting achievements were, the Party asserted, an attractive inducement to others to raise their standards and participate; further, if the USSR were to compete internationally—and the resolution stated that

sporting contacts between worker-athletes of the Soviet Union and other countries help to fortify even more the international workers' front.[9]

—it required a mass basis on which to draw for its resources to attain a high level of performance.

This, then, was the definitive statement on the rôle of sport in Soviet society to which all subsequent policy statements were to refer. We have already seen that sport, having become the responsibility of the health ministry, was employed as a means of inculcating standards of hygiene and regular exercise in a predominantly socially-backward peasant country. Its therapeutic value, was for example, widely advertised in the intermittent three-day antituberculosis campaigns of the late 1920s. It was also not thought incongruous to put out a poster ostensibly advertising sports, yet featuring a young man with a rifle and toothbrush above the slogan "Clean Your Teeth! Clean Your Rifle!"

But sport was not confined to improving *physical* health; it was regarded as important in combating anti-social and anti-Soviet be-haviour in town and country. If urban young people, especially, could be persuaded to take up sport and engage in regular physical exercise, they might develop healthy bodies *and* minds. Thus, the Ukrainian Party Central Committee issued a resolution in 1926 expressing the hope that

physical culture would become the vehicle of the new life . . . a means of
isolating young people from the evil influence of the street, home-made
liquor and prostitution.[10]

The rôle assigned sport in the countryside was even more ambitious:
it was

to play a big part in the campaign against drunkenness and uncivilised behaviour
by attracting village youth to more sensible and cultured activities . . . In the
fight to transform the village, physical culture is to be a vehicle of the new way
of life in all measures undertaken by the Soviet authorities—in the fight against
religion and natural calamities.[11]

Sport, then, stood for "clean-living", progress, good health and rationality and was regarded by the Party as one of the most suitable and
effective instruments for implementing its social policies.

The far-reaching aims envisaged for sport may be illustrated by the
early concern that physical culture should make some contribution to
the social emancipation of women—in Soviet society generally, and
especially in the Muslim areas where women were effectively excluded
from all public life. As was made clear,

In Uzbekistan, as in other Central Asian republics, women's path to sport has
been linked with a struggle against religious prejudices and for equal status in
society.[12]

The bodily liberation and naked limbs (and faces!), along with the
self-acting, competing "image" associated with sport (as, for example
personified in the graceful Tartar gymnasts Elvira Saadi and Nelli
Kim) have not been accepted without a struggle:

I would call our first sportswomen real heroines. They accomplished real feats
of valour in liberating women from the age-old yoke of religion and the
feudal-bey order.[13]

Even in the European areas of the country, the women's emancipation-
through-sport policy was presented as both feasible and effective. For
example, in a letter to Podvoisky through the medium of Pravda in
1922, the first women graduates from the Central Military School of
Workers' Physical Culture wrote:

You understand how important physical culture is for women and you tried to
impress its importance upon us women, among whom there is so much
passivity and conservatism, the results of age-old servitude, both economic
and social.[14]

To sum up, there existed during the 1920s a widespread idealistic
adherence to the notion of a "healthy mind in a healthy body", a
feeling that physical culture could somehow be used, along with other
policies, to combat socially and politically undesirable phenomena.

(iii) *Sport against the background of industrialisation 1929–41*

Towards the end of the NEP period, the economy was getting back on its feet: in the economic year 1925/6, industrial production had reached 90 per cent of its 1913 level. The scene was thus set for the implementation of an industrialisation programme that was to hurl the whole of the country into a gigantic campaign to "build socialism", then to lead to the forcible collectivisation of agriculture and transform the USSR from a backward agrarian into an advanced industrial, if unbalanced, economy. The First Five-Year Plan went into operation on 1 October 1928 on a scale and with planning that more resembled a military campaign than peace-time construction.

The implications for the sports movement of these economic processes were extremely important, for it was in the 1930s that the pattern of Soviet sport as we know it today was principally formed and its main rôle and explicit functions in society were set. If the previous decade may be described as having been dominated by physical culture the 1930s were to be a decade of competitive sport.

The first step was to set up, on 3 April 1930, the All-Union Physical Culture Council—a ministry for sport, in effect—with powers to decide all issues concerning the organisation of sport. The second step taken by the Party was to transfer all primary sports clubs to local workplaces. In future, all local sports clubs were to be organised on a production basis, all the people belonging to a particular factory, office or college (and members of their families) being eligible for membership of the sports "collective" at their place of work.

Sport, therefore, now had a powerful central organisational nucleus in the form of the All-Union Council—which was to exist with only relatively minor changes until 1959. At the other end of the scale, there were active and politically-controllable sports groups directly at places of work and cultural and educational centres. In other words, sport was brought into line with the standard pattern for all activities at the time, becoming a hierarchical state organisation. By the mid-1930s, however, the sports movement had become more complex. It was one thing getting employees to joing trade-union sports collectives, but it was quite another sustaining their interest by arranging contests with other workplace teams. There was the problem, too, of what to do about (and even how to discover) proficient athletes: how best to train them and arrange top-flight competition for them. It was therefore decided in 1935 to set up trade-union based voluntary sports societies. The factory collectives were to remain at workplace level as the primary links in the sports movement, but now they were to come under a specific trade-union sports society. In March 1935, the first society Spartak was formed. Shortly after, sports societies of individual trade-unions were formed: Lokomotiv, representing railway workers, Torpedo, representing car workers, Stroitel' (Builder) representing construction workers and several others. These were similar in structure to that of the Dinamo Society, which had been established by the security services in 1923.

The formation of the sports societies—which were to be an important link in the whole sports movement right up to the present day—confirmed the production principle of primary organisation in that since Soviet trade unions are organised on an industry-by-industry basis, so too are the sports societies. Each society was to have its own rules, membership-cards, badge and colours. It was to be financed out of trade-union dues and other funds and given the responsibility for building large sports amenities, acquiring equipment and sportswear for its members and maintaining a permanent staff of coaches, instructors and medical personnel. Members have the right to use the club's equipment and facilities free of charge, elect and be elected to its steering bodies.

One of the main tasks of the sports societies was to act as a catalyst in raising standards through more rational organisation and competition: they were more direct "transmission belts" to sportsmen than had previously existed. Contests were to be conducted on an intra- and inter-society and territorial basis. Each society had its local, regional, Republican and All-Union championships for each sport it practised. The selection of sports-society teams at all levels was founded on these competitions. This system of contests led to the creation of nation-wide sports leagues and cup competitions for such popular games as soccer, basketball and ice-hockey. Until 1935, All-Union championships had been contested by city teams; in 1936, however, the All-Union Soccer League and Cup competition were both instituted. Societies such as Dinamo, Spartak, Torpedo and Lokomotiv had so-called "teams of masters" in every major town, some of which competed in one of the various leagues. These leagues created new interest and mass appeal, especially in the most popular male team-game, soccer, and drew many thousands of spectators to view important matches.

Acknowledgement of the importance of competitive sport came with a government decision in June 1937 to award the country's top distinction, the Order of Lenin, to the Dinamo and Spartak sports societies. The previous year, some fifty athletes had been awarded medals and various orders. This was the first time that individual sportsmen had featured in the "honours list", which was some indication of the official "solicitude" (and public adulation) that heroes and shock-workers in sport—like individuals who excelled in other spheres—were accorded in the "cult" period.

The formation of the voluntary sports societies and the increasing numbers of participants led to a review of the motivational provisions in sport. Thus, two important elements of the Soviet sports system to give people clear-cut targets of achievement were instituted in the 1930s. The first, the *Gotov k trudu i oborone—GTO* (Ready for Labour and Defence) programme, was intended to achieve two aims:

(*a*) to extend the scope of sports participation, give everyone something to aim for—i.e. set modest targets whose attainment brought some official honorific recognition—and start to make regular participation in sport a normal feature of "the socialist way of life". The targets were to be not for a single sport, nor even for sporting ability alone, but for all-round ability in a number of sports and knowledge of the rudiments of hygiene, first-aid and physical educational theory.

(*b*) to establish a mass base from which potential "stars" could be drawn. Once the stars were discovered, it was necessary to categorise and institutionalise them according to their level of ability in a particular sport and to give them an incentive and amenities to realise their potential. For this purpose a second element was introduced into the system: a uniform rankings system for individual sports, setting four levels of superior achievement. These four rankings were decided by times recorded in a particular event and/or success in competition, both national and international. Figure 1 illustrates this combined GTO rankings pyramid as it exists today.

The decision taken in the mid-1930s to stratify in sport, to distinguish a more or less professional group of sportsmen from the main body, was in keeping with the country's social development and its concomitant official values: in industry and agriculture, reward and prestige went to the *peredoviki*—the workers and teams that attained the best results. The ordinary people were to be inspired by the efforts of people with whom they could identify.

To sum up, with the embarking of the USSR onto a course of rapid industrialisation, the pattern of sport for the new society began to take shape. By the end of the 1930s, the basic organisational pattern had already been set—with its sports societies, primary sports collectives, sports schools, GTO programmes and uniform rankings system. The Soviet society of the 1930s differed from that of the preceding period in seeing the flourishing of all manner of competitive sports (soccer, basketball, volleyball) with mass spectator appeal and the official encouragement of leagues, stadiums, cups, championships, popularity-polls, cults of sporting heroes—all the appendages of a sub-system designed to provide general recreation for the fast-growing urban populace. It has to be remembered that one of the most profound social consequences of industrialisation was the very rapid shift of people from country to town.[15] Millions of people, uprooted from centuries-old traditions, were pitched into new and strange environ-

Figure I.   THE USSR SPORTS AWARD PYRAMID

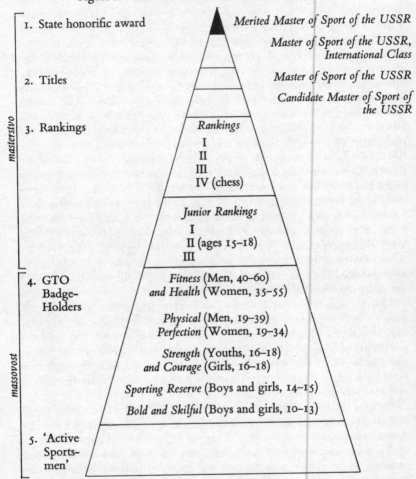

1. State honorific award — *Merited Master of Sport of the USSR*

Master of Sport of the USSR, International Class

2. Titles — *Master of Sport of the USSR*

Candidate Master of Sport of the USSR

3. Rankings — *Rankings*
I
II
III
IV (chess)

Junior Rankings
I
II (ages 15–18)
III

4. GTO Badge-Holders — *Fitness* (Men, 40–60) *and Health* (Women, 35–55)

Physical (Men, 19–39) *Perfection* (Women, 19–34)

Strength (Youths, 16–18) *and Courage* (Girls, 16–18)

Sporting Reserve (Boys and girls, 14–15)

Bold and Skilful (Boys and girls, 10–13)

5. 'Active Sports-men'

masterstvo

massovost

N.B. The two top titles are honorary for life. The only higher award to which an outstanding and internationally-successful athlete may aspire is Merited Master of Sport of the USSR, but this is a state honorific decoration outside the classification system. Sports rankings are awarded for results achieved in official Soviet competition and are valid for two years only. The physical token of having gained one of the titles or rankings is a badge and certificate, although recipients also receive preference in admission to sports schools and physical education colleges. In chess and draughts the title *Grandmaster of the USSR* is the equivalent of Master of Sport of the USSR, International Class for other sports.

ments and found themselves building vast ironworks and blast-furnaces in previously uninhabited wastes like Magnitogorsk, oil refineries and pipelines in the Caucasus or railways across the deserts of Turkestan, working on the new collective farms or even, indeed, in the labour camps of Siberia. This social upheaval was bound to have a reflection on the nature of and requirements for sporting activity. Besides pouring into factories, the newcomers to industry joined factory clubs and looked to them for the recreation they had previously enjoyed in an open-air rural setting. Since urban living conditions were spartan and deteriorating,[16] sports served many townsmen as an escape from the drudgery of their domestic and work environments. The many sports-parades and pageants which constituted a background to the sports contests of the 1930s were intended, too, to create and reinforce a "togetherness", to evoke feelings of patriotism, and to demonstrate to people (abroad as well as at home) how happy and carefree life was under socialism in the USSR—"under the sun of the Stalin Constitution", as it was said after 1936. It is significant that sports rallies often accompanied major political events or festivals (May Day, Constitution Day and the Anniversary of the October Revolution). This practice began with the *Vsevobuch* parade to mark the fourth anniversary of the Revolution in 1921, but it became general only in the 1930s. In this way, sport became a means of linking members of the public with politics, the Party and, of course, Stalin (his portrait, in hundreds of copies, deputising for his person—since he preferred to cultivate the image of himself as a remote godhead).

Finally, a relatively close link was re-established between sport and the military. It stemmed partly from the leaders' conviction of the need for a state surrounded by unfriendly powers to be strong militarily and constantly on the alert. This conviction became widespread in the "besieged fortress" atmosphere of the 1930s, encouraged in part by the rise of fascism in Europe and by the deliberate playing up of the danger from without (and from the "enemy agents" within) to justify the hardships and sacrifice which the intensive industrialisation campaign entailed. Sport openly became a means of providing premilitary training and achieving a relatively high standard of national fitness for defence. Several sports with potential military applications—e.g. skiing, shooting, gliding and mountain-climbing—came to be dominated by servicemen, The two largest and most successful clubs in the country were those run by the armed forces and the security forces: the Central House of the Red Army and Dinamo.[17] And, after 1931, the GTO sports system was expressly intended to train people, through sport, for work and military preparedness.

(iv) *Supreme test of physical training 1941–45*

The Soviet involvement in the Second World War lasted from June 1941 to August 1945. Hitler's armies struck deep into the country to the very outskirts of Moscow and Leningrad before they were driven out. They left behind them great areas of devastation in the west of the country, including most of European Russia. Loss of life was officially estimated at over 20 millions.

The war years cannot simply be seen as a wasted interlude that retarded the sports movement. They had certain consequences, some intangible, but nonetheless quite far-reaching, whose effect was evident for many years ahead.

(a) The war convinced the authorities that they had been absolutely right to "functionalise" sport and make countrywide physical fitness a prime target.

(b) It reinforced a belief in a military bias in physical training and sport. After the war, the rôle of military organisations like the army sports clubs, Dinamo and the civil defence organisation DOSAAF was to be enhanced and these institutions made the organisational pillars of the whole sports movement. A national physical-fitness programme was to be the principal goal, and sports with explicit military utility were to become compulsory in all educational establishments and sports societies.

(c) The emotional effect of the war on Soviet people was capitalised on by the holding of sports festivals named after eminent athletes who had died in the war. Even though virtually everyone had lost a close relative, a *national* grief could be evoked at the loss of a popular sporting hero. The names and memory of these were now to be invoked both for keeping the memory of the war alive in people's minds and for drawing people to sport:

Sports contests for prizes dedicated to the memory of outstanding athletes and heroes of the Great Patriotic War are of special significance. They are very important educationally both for the sportsmen and for the spectators.[18]

(d) Victory in the war gave the Soviet people a sense of pride in their achievements, a feeling that the period of pre-war industrialisation and sacrifice had been justified. Now they could take on the world in another—peaceful—form of contest, in sport, and test their potential. But the war had been won at a price; many Soviet people felt that they had borne the brunt of German might and had made untold sacrifices to free the world from the blight of fascism. The resultant feelings of patriotism were to be an evident part of the motivation for victory in foreign competition after the war.

(v) *Restoration and consolidation 1945-58*

Although the war had brought German invasion and extensive damage to the Soviet Union, it also brought Soviet influence into the heart of Europe—a source of seemingly interminable friction with the Western Powers. In these conditions of international conflict and economic devastation, the Soviet people had to turn to the task of reconstruction which, once again, had to be accomplished largely from the country's own resources. Peace, in fact, brought no relenting in either economic tempos or political pressures. This inevitably had its effect on social policies and social life, not least of all on Soviet sport.

With the conclusion of the war and the setting of a new national target—to catch up and overtake the most advanced industrial powers (and that included catching up and overtaking in sport)—the pre-war pyramidal structure of sports administration had to be re-established and refurbished to suit the new circumstances. Furthermore, it became evident that if the USSR were to compete internationally, it would have to join existing international federations and comply with their rules. Since most of these bodies had been set up for "amateur" sportsmen at the end of the nineteenth century and their definitions and rules reflected in sport the social distinctions then current in society, they laid down quite stringent rules about remuneration of competitors in each amateur sport and the maximum amount of time they were to devote to that pursuit. Despite the Soviet distaste for the kind of social privilege reflected in bourgeois "amateur" status, Soviet sportsmen had to play the game according to these rules if they were to play at all against the world's best athletes. The appearance, at least, then, had to be given that they complied with the definition of an "amateur". The problems of money and occuptation had to be solved.

First, in July 1947, the USSR Council of Ministers issued a special resolution "On Remuneration of the Sporting Attainments of Soviet Sportsmen" in which it reversed its earlier prescription of monetary rewards (for setting records and winning championships)[19] and now declared that the only awards to be made for national and world records were to be gold and silver medals and silver and bronze badges.[20]

Second, it was asserted that henceforth there were no professional entertainers in Soviet sport in the sense that there were strong social and official sanctions which prevented sport from interfering with an athlete's all-round development and his success in a non-sporting vocation. There had always been, it was pointed out, an elaborate apparatus for facilitating the physical and talent development of every sports enthusiast (for example, all competitors, if qualifying, got expenses and leave).

It transpired that proficient sportsmen would be following one of three occupations: student, servicemen or P.E. instructor, under the sponsorship of a trade-union or other (such as Dinamo or army) sports society. A master sportsman—i.e., one who more or less devotes a major part of his time to training for and playing a sport during his active career as a sportsman (officially, this person would be said to devote his time to "teaching" and "organising")—is paid by his sports society according to his ranking, results and several other factors. This enables him to devote much time to sport (unencumbered by a job of work outside sport, but not free from academic studies and certain social obligations) and to be coached under the auspices of and using the facilities of the society. In the case of the country's two best endowed sports societies, Dinamo and the Central Army Sports Club, he would normally hold a commission but not be expected to undergo any form of military service.

The stage was now set to qualify for international contests and to take on the best in the world. In December 1948, the Party Central Committee set the targets in a resolution that made it clear that im-proved proficiency could and should be based on mass participation; it called on all interested parties—sports committees, the Komsomol, trade unions and Party organisations everywhere

to spread sport to every corner of the land, to raise the level of skill and, on that basis, to help Soviet sportsmen win world supremacy in the major sports in the immediate future.[21]

The "world supremacy" target was something new to the sports movement and flatly contradicted the condemnation of "record-mania" that the Party had made in its pre-war pronouncements. But it reflected the social trends in the country and the popular mood after the war, and was not greatly dissimilar from the contemporary aims—though these were not always so explicity stated—of other great sporting nations, particularly since the Cold War was increasingly dividing the world into two opposing camps, vying for influence over the rest of humanity.

The Party resolution outlined a specific programme for attaining the targets it had set; it entailed reinforcing the organisation of sports-collectives; ensuring the all-round expansion of all sports but with particular attention given to Olympic sports; improving the sports amenities; bringing Master's and other ranking standards into line with international records; setting up sports schools; heightening the re-sponsibility of coaches for the performance of their charges (by awarding them bonuses for high attainments by their athletes); and extensively utilising the press, radio and cinema for popularising sport among the public.

Before the war, apart from the sports-exchanges between the USSR and Nazi Germany and the Baltic States in 1940, few official representatives of foreign states had visited the Soviet Union for a sporting event, nor had Soviet athletes competed, except on rare occasions, with athletes other than those belonging to workers' sports associations. Nor had Soviet sports associations joined or been invited to join international federations. Further, since tsarist Russia's participation in the 1912 Olympics, no Russian or Soviet team had contested the Games.[22] That is not to say that standards in Soviet sport were necessarily inferior to those in the West. It is claimed that, by 1939, forty-four Soviet records bettered world records, including twenty-three in weightlifting, nine in athletics, nine in pistol shooting, two in swimming and one in speed skating.[23] They could not be registered, of course, because the USSR was not a member of international federations.

In the immediate post-war years, Soviet sports associations affiliated to nearly all the major international sports federations and Soviet athletes were competing regularly at home and abroad against foreign opposition. The Soviet Olympic Committee was formed in May 1951 and the USSR made its Olympic début at the Fifteenth Games, held in Helsinki, in 1952.

The rising proficiency standards after the war led, in the main, to the desired results in international contests, though by no means in all sports—despite the attempt to cultivate all the sports in the Olympic programme. Some sports, like weightlifting, wrestling, speed skating, gymnastics and chess—in which Soviet sportsmen had established world dominance by the early 1950s—were based on long-standing traditions in that particular sport and top achievements were attained partly through wide participation. Some sports, like athletics and the team-games of soccer, basketball and volleyball, were of more recent vintage and to some extent depend on sophisticated equipment and regular top-class competition; nevertheless, they seem to have had quite a wide base and, despite the handicaps, Soviet athletes performed remarkably well in their initial international contests—mostly on a par with the leading players of other nations. In sports without national tradition and popular support which required intensive training with relatively modern and complex installations—motor-racing, tennis, swimming, ski-jumping, slalom, cycling and yachting—Soviet sportsmen either refrained from international competition altogether during the 1950s or performed very moderately. The extent of Soviet success in the Olympic Games may be seen in Table 1. Despite some sporting setbacks, there is certainly ample evidence to show that the USSR has gone a considerable way to achieving its aim of world supremacy in sport, "winning" every Olympic Games, summer and winter, with the sole exception of 1968.

Table 1.   USSR PERFORMANCE IN THE OLYMPIC GAMES 1952–76

| | Summer Games | | | | | | Winter Games | | | | | |
| | | | | | Nearest Rival | | | | | | Nearest Rival | |
Year	Gold Medals	Medal Total	Points[a]	Position	Medals	Points	Gold Medals	Medal Total	Points	Position	Medals	Points
1952	22	71	494	1	76	494[c]	—[b]	—[b]	—[b]	—[b]	—[b]	—[b]
1956	37	98	624·5	1	74	498[c]	7	16	103	1	11	66·5[d]
1960	43	103	683	1	71	463·5[c]	7	21	146·5	1	7	62·5[e]
1964	30	96	608·3	2	90	581·8[c]	11	25	183	1	15	89·3[f]
1968	29	91	591·5	1	106	709[c]	5	13	92	2	14	103[f]
1972	50	99	665·5	1	93	636·5[c]	8	16	120	1	14	83[g]
1976	47	125	788·5	1	92	606[c]	13	27	201	1	19	138[g]

[a] The points-allocation is that used in the *Olympic Bulletin*: awarding seven points for first place, five for second and so on down to one point for sixth place, i.e.

Placing	1	2	3	4	5	6
Points awarded	7	5	4	3	2	1

[b] USSR not participating
[c] USA   [d] Austria   [e] Sweden   [f] Norway   [g] East Germany

Partly in line with industrial reorganisation and partly to adapt its sports structure to new policies, the sports administration adopted a new pattern of trade-union sports societies at the end of 1957: the All-Union Council of Trade Unions resolved to dissolve its ninety-nine sports societies and combine them into a single society for all employees in industry and construction for each of the 15 Republics, regardless of union affiliation—i.e., on a territorial basis. Within each Republic, the Republican Council of Trade Unions had to choose the name of its society: in the Russian Republic, it was Trud–Labour, in the Ukraine, it was Avangard, in Latvia—Daugava, and so on. A separate rural sports society was also to be set up in each Republic. At the time of this reorganisation in 1957, two All-Union trade-union sports societies were left intact: Lokomotiv for all railway workers, and Vodnik for river and canal transport employees. Further, an All-Union students' sports society was set up—Burevestnik. Three years later, in 1960, Spartak came under trade-union authority and became a fourth All-Union sports society (for people employed in health, civil service, trade, food, culture, education, etc.). That made thirty-four trade-union sports societies in all. Two non-trade-union societies were Dinamo and Labour Reserves. The only sports organisations that did not come within this category of voluntary sports society were the army sports clubs, DOSAAF and the Hunters' Society.

All the sports groups came together for the biggest domestic sporting event of the 1950s: the First Spartakiad of the Peoples of the USSR, whose final was held in Moscow in mid-August 1956. The Soviet government had previously instructed every sports group in the country every district, region, town, village and Republican sports organisation to prepare for the event, hold qualifying contests, construct the requisite facilities and make the forthcoming games the biggest and most widely publicised sports occasion in the country's history. It was to be, too, the forerunner of regular sports festivals to be held every four years in the year preceding the Olympic Games; it was also a much-publicised demonstration of the mass (and especially the multi-national) nature and the excellence of the Soviet sports movement. It is claimed that as many as 23 million people took part in the contests leading up to the finals. As a means of popularising sport and organising tests of skill, the games certainly did their job.[24]

The finals were held in the newly-opened Lenin Stadium on the banks of the Moscow River at the foot of Lenin Hills, with seating in the main stadium for 104,000 spectators. The importance of the occasion was marked by the presence of all prominent Party leaders and a number of eminent foreign guests including the presidents of many international federations and the then president of the IOC (Avery Brundage).

As an event the Spartakiad was certainly unsurpassed in the history of Soviet sport. It was intended to be exactly that: an event of political and social significance in the lives of Soviet people. It was not merely a taking stock of Soviet sports achievements and a launching-pad for the coming Olympic Games, it was also meant to be a culturally unifying force; the authorities relied on the popularity of sport to bring together representatives and ordinary people from all sections of Soviet society in a festive, patriotic mood on a great occasion organised by Party and State. Further, attempts were made then and since to present sport as something ennobling, a cultural force that enriches man's experience. Emphasis is put on the mass gymnastics and formation-displays as art forms, thereby highlighting the aesthetic element.

To sum up, having proved itself militarily at enormous cost in the war, the Soviet leadership now felt the need to prove itself in non-military spheres—which it was becoming capable of doing. Given the limited opportunities elsewhere, sport seemed to offer a suitable medium for pursuing this goal. This was an area in which the USSR did not have to take second place to the West. The Soviet citizen was therefore encouraged to identify team-loyalty with state-loyalty; sport acted as a force tending to legitimate the Soviet system in the eyes of the citizen. Of course, this policy presupposed a level of skill in a wide range of sports superior to that existing in the leading Western states. On the eve of the war, Soviet sport was approaching this level in several sports; in some, it had actually reached it. This trend was strengthened after the war by mobilising the total (if limited) resources of the entire sports-system, by encouraging more or less full-time, well-remunerated sportsmen and teams, and by concentrating the best resources on them.

(vi) Modern urban life and leisure

Since the late 1950s, there has been a fairly steady increase in public and personal prosperity, a marked growth in the range and quantity of consumer goods available, a reduction in working time and a continuing shift in population-balance in favour of the towns (the urban population first exceeded the rural in 1961). All these factors are having a qualitative effect on the pattern of recreation—which, in turn, is having social and political consequences for society as a whole.

(a) Increasing prosperity. Figures published in the USSR indicate that both national income and consumption have more than doubled since 1960. Part of the increased personal income and consumption is un-doubtedly being spent on recreation and sport, on the pursuit of a growing variety of activities, particularly outdoor ones, and on personal durables such as skis, skates, tennis and badminton rackets, fishing tackle, tents and, to a lesser extent, on motor cycles, canoes, dinghies, yachts and cars.[25] This would seem clearly to be a long-term trend.

Higher national income has also resulted in more substantial government allocation to sports facilities and the development of a number of activities that presuppose a certain level of industrial development and economic surplus.[26]

(b) *Increasing free time*. The relationship of work to leisure has also altered radically in the last two decades.[27] Not merely has there been an increase in the amount of leisure-time but the reduction in the workday has resulted in workers spending less time than previously in such well-defined institutional settings as factory and office. The breakthrough that signals the greatest revolution in the pattern of recreation, just as in other advanced industrial societies, was the introduction in March 1967 of the long weekend. The boom in camping, fishing, hunting, rock-climbing, pot-holing, water-skiing, motoring and boating is partly accounted for by longer holidays with pay and partly by the developing cult of the weekend.

(c) *Increasing urbanisation*. Over half the Soviet population now lives in a relatively modern, urban, industrial society,[28] a human condition which, in itself, regardless of political values and policies, predisposes people to certain kinds of recreational activities. At the same time as people have migrated to the towns, the government has followed a policy of high-density building in multi-storey blocks of flats. Despite the fact that in the Soviet Union town-planning tends to allow for sizeable courtyard facilities for each block of flats, the problem of providing adequate outdoor amenities for sport is becoming ever greater in the most densely-settled urban areas.

Thus, rising personal prosperity, an increasing amount of free time, particularly the long weekend, and the pressures of an urban-industrial environment, have certain implications for sport. For example, people are tending to form smaller (family) groups for recreation and holidays. There appears to be an increasing desire to "get away from it all" rather than to "get together". In the past, the leadership has, on the whole, tried to see to it that the facilities available to the population at large predispose them toward some form of public, collective recreation—mainly through the sports club, workplace, trade-union, public park or play-centre behind a block of flats. Now that most workers have a long weekend away from work, these production-based facilities no longer suit them. There is, therefore, a trend away from "public and mass" sports activities towards "individual, domestic, family and passive" leisure—especially watching television. "Televiewing" has, in fact, become the single most important time-consuming leisure activity.[29]

One increasing problem for the authorities has been to see that this additional free time is used in a *rational* way, that leisure should be socially functional. Well-spent time on sports activities is held to be important because of the contribution it makes to production and the smooth functioning of society in general. It should enrich the individual so that he may enrich society. Despite the toleration of a whole range of activities that appear to be at odds with notions of rationality— horse-racing, as a spectator'sport for gamblers at the various hippo-dromes in big Soviet cities, dominoes, lotto (bingo) and many card games—others have been attacked and sometimes proscribed because of their alleged "irrationality" or exhibitionist nature or for the fact that they lend themselves to commercial exploitation. Such activities include women's soccer and wrestling, male body-building, yoga, karate and bridge—all of which were condemned in a government resolution of January 1973.

One can understand the official disquiet at such spectacles as women's soccer and wrestling being arranged for male voyeuristic enjoyment given the ideological disapproval of hedonistic sex and displays of public sexuality. Both women's soccer and wrestling were condemned be-cause they

aroused unhealthy excitement among some spectators . . . and are harmful to a woman's organism in that they may cause damage to sexual functions, varicose veins, thrombophlebitis, etc.[30]

It has been particularly difficult to keep male body-building within state-desired limits. With an eye to the "excesses" that exist in the West, the authorities fear it will become an excuse for exhibitionism and narcissism:

Egotistic love and dandified culture of the body are alien to the Soviet system of physical culture and sport which cultivates collectivism and aspires to bring as much good to society as possible.[31]

Oriental pursuits such as yoga and karate have been attacked because of their association with a philosophy that is alien to that of Soviet society:

Yoga is based not on the cognition of objective laws of reality and their use in practice, rather it leads to religion and mysticism.[32]

This criticism is also levelled at karate.

Card games have regularly been animadverted on throughout Soviet history as time-wasting, empty activities often associated with gambling and luck, so it was no surprise to see bridge condemned in 1973 as a "perversion" of well-spent leisure activities. No official reason was given, but one may surmise that the game was regarded as a potential menace to productivity, as an "irrational" use of free time.

All the above-mentioned "sports" had gained a hold, it was claimed, because of the connivance, acquiescence and unprincipled activity of certain administrators. Instead of properly organising the free time of workers, they became involved in

charlatanism and roguery, helping to implant and popularise all manner of "fashionable" exercises designed to excite people and encourage a spirit of profit that is detrimental to the health of participants and, to a certain extent, causes social harm to Soviet society.[33]

The emphasis on the special interdependence of work and games stems from the paramount importance attributed to work and from the claim that, in socialist society, it has acquired a uniquely satisfactory character owing to the absence of exploitation and alienation. Yet, as with other media of recreation and leisure—e.g. television and the cinema—the official descriptions must be understood as arising largely from a desire to *educate* the public in the broad sense of the word and to prevent the wasteful dissipation of energy and time.

At the same time, with more money, more free time and a wider range of recreation to choose from, Soviet people are increasingly able to select the sporting activity that most accords with their personal desire and aspiration. With improved facilities and opportunities, participation in sport is becoming less ruled by the official utilitarian-instrumental approach and more governed by the notion that a game, a sport or outdoor activity of any kind is desirable in itself, for its own sake.

Concern over efforts to regulate the increasing free time, and not merely to provide facilities for its use, however, led to a number of important organisational changes during the 1960s in sport. The most outstanding were contained in a Party and government resolution of 11 August 1966 "On Measures to Promote Physical Culture and Sport", which obliged all Party central committees and Republican governments, trade union and Komsomol organisations, and all sports bodies to improve administration of the sports movement and to take all measures to promote sport so that it would become a more active means by which society could influence people's moral outlook, encourage their all-round harmonious development and highly-productive labour, would help them maintain their health and remain creative until old age, and would prepare them for defence of their country.[34]

Not since the 1925 Party resolution on sport had the utilitarian and social functions of Soviet sport been spelled out so tersely; for several years to come, hardly any official article on sport would go into print without due acknowledgement of the "August Resolutions" of 1966, as they became known. The resolutions were strong meat and put sport on the agenda, for the first time, of many Party Committee meetings. The highlight of the resolutions was the desire to make sport universal, a part of the everyday life of all men and women, young and old. A target of 60 million people regularly and actively engaged in sport was set for 1970.

Two years later, on 1 October 1968, the sports movement was taken under more direct government control with the creation of the All-Union Committee on Physical Culture and Sport attached to the Council of Ministers of the USSR. The new Committee's resolutions on sport were to be binding on all ministries and public organisations. Similar sports committees were set up in each of the fifteen republics. The new Chairman was Sergei Pavlov, an experienced Party man, who had been Secretary of the Central Committee of the Komsomol from 1959 to 1968.

At the same time as the campaign was launched to draw more people into sport, attempts were made to improve proficiency by setting up centres of excellence or sports boarding schools (see below).

At the beginning of this period, in the late 1950s, sport was, for the vast majority of Soviet people, a matter of physical exercise performed at home, school or work, a game of dominoes in the backyard with neighbours and, perhaps, a visit to a soccer stadium or ice-hockey rink. For the casual sportsman, facilities for pursuing most sports were few. By the 1970s, however, although many Soviet people still took no greater interest in sport than watching an occasional match on television or reading the daily sports newspaper, the opportunities were present for fairly wide-ranging sports participation. It would appear that many young people in towns were, in fact, availing themselves of these facilities and engaging in sports, often inspired by the glamour of thrilling performances, especially against foreign opposition. By virtue of its far-flung and well-integrated nature, sport has today become an institution of considerable social importance.

II. Sport and physical education in school and college

(i) P.E. and games in schools

Physical education is an integral part of education and serves to ensure the all-round development of the physical and moral qualities of schoolchildren, to prepare them for life, labour and defence of their country. More specifically, physical education should strengthen health, develop physical skills, the functional potential of the organism and motor skills, and inculcate moral qualities such as patriotism, internationalism, team-work, boldness, purposefulness, perseverance and self-assurance.

(Statute on School Physical Education ratified by USSR Ministry of Education and Committee on Physical Culture and Sport attached to USSR Council of Ministers, February 2, 1971.)[35]

Of course, such aims are not the monopoly of Soviet schools; similar aims are proclaimed, for example, in Britain and the USA, although here society's dominant values of individualism, acquisitiveness, competitiveness and "unity in diversity" also find a reflection in socialisation, often at variance with those values proclaimed in school, including P.E. Such a conflict does not occur in Soviet society, where a single set of standards is presented and reinforced largely by social pressure.

Soviet schools, then, differ from their Western counterparts in (a) the explicitness and directness of the application of their aims to practise, and (b) their standardisation of curricula and syllabuses. Thus, a detailed syllabus is laid down by the USSR Ministry of Education which is compulsory for all teachers to follow. In a highly centralised society like the Soviet Union's it seems normal to have a single syllabus imposed from above. Schooling begins for all Soviet children at seven years of age and extends over ten years. P.E. lessons, in forty-five-minute periods, are generally held separately for boys and girls. Of the total school curriculum of thirty-six hours per week, two periods are, on average, devoted to physical education (including games). In some republics, three to four periods are devoted. Homework is officially prescribed for the subject, twice a week, to last some fifteen minutes on each occasion; a child may be kept down if he fails his end-of-year P.E. examination, and the subject features in the school-leaving certificate.

The syllabus introduced in 1967 for Soviet schools consisted in the following:

Table 2. P.E. AND GAMES LESSONS PER SCHOOL YEAR, CLASSES 1-10

Class	Age	Gymnastics	Athletics	Skiing	Team Games*	Total
1	7+	28	—	12	30	70
2	8	30	—	12	28	70
3-4	9-10	36	—	12	22	70
5-6	11-12	19	19	14	18	70
7-8	13-14	20	20	14	16	70
9-10	15-17	19	19	14	18	70

* Mainly basketball and volleyball

With the launching of the new "Ready for Labour and Defence" programme in 1972, however, the P.E. syllabus in all Soviet schools was required to be based upon it. Every school has a target to reach in respect of sports-involvement and sports-standards to which it is hoped its children will aspire. The target in 1970 was for every fit 14-15 year-

Table 3.   GTO STAGE 3 FOR BOYS AND GIRLS AGED 16–18

1. To have a knowledge of "Physical Culture and Sport in the USSR".

2. To know and carry out rules for personal and public hygiene.

3. To be able to carry out the initial military training programme, to wear a gas-mask for one hour, to know the basic rules of civil defence.

4. To be able to explain the importance of and to perform a set of morning exercises.

5. To perform the following exercises within the given standards:

Type of Exercise	Boys		Girls	
	Silver	Gold	Silver	Gold
1. Run 100m (sec)	14·2	13·5	16·2	15·4
2. Run 500m (min/sec)	—	—	2·00	1·50
Run 1000m (min/sec)	3·30	3·20	—	—
or Skate 500m (min/sec)	1·25	1·15	1·30	1·20
3. Long jump (cm)	440	480	340	375
or High jump (cm)	125	135	105	115
4. Hurl handgrenade				
of 500gm (m)	—	—	21	25
of 700gm (m)	35	40	—	—
or putt the shot				
of 4kg (cm)	—	—	600	680
of 5kg (cm)	800	1000	—	—
5. Ski 3km (min)	—	—	20	18
5km (min)	27	25	—	—
or 10km (min)	57	52	—	—
In snow-free areas:				
Run cross-country				
3km (min)	—	—	30	27
6km (min)	35	32	—	—
or Cycle cross-country				
10km (min)	—	—	30	27
6. Swim 100m (min/sec)	2·00	1·45	2·15	2·00
7. Press-ups	8	12	—	—
Pull-ups	—	—	10	12

Type of Exercise	Boys		Girls	
	Silver	Gold	Silver	Gold
8. Fire a small-bore rifle at 25m (points)	33	40	30	37
or at 50m	30	37	27	34
or Fire a heavy weapon	satis.	well	satis.	well
9. Tourist hike with tests and orienteering	1 of 20km or 2 of 12km	1 of 25km or 2 of 15km	1 of 20km or 2 of 12km	1 of 25km or 2 of 15km
10. Obtain a sports-rank:	—	3rd	—	3rd
(a) motor-car, motor-boat, motor-cycle, gliding, parachuting, aeroplane, water-sports, biathlon, pentathlon, pistol shooting, orienteering, boxing or wrestling;				
(b) any other sport	2nd	—	2nd	—

N.B. For the Gold badge, one has to complete not less than 7 qualifying standards at Gold-badge level and 2 standards at Silver-badge level (except item 10). Girls who have completed a first-aid training course may forego item 10 for their Gold badge.

old to gain a GTO badge and a third junior ranking in a particular sport, for every 16-17 year-old to obtain the appropriate GTO badge and at least a second junior ranking in a sport, and for at least 20 per cent of all 15-17 year olds to obtain the third adult ranking in a particular sport.[36] Schools I visited in Moscow and Leningrad in the mid-1970s were, in fact, centring their P.E. programme on the appropriate GTO requirements. It will therefore be useful to examine one of the relevant five stages of the Ready for Labour and Defence national fitness programme (see Table 3.)

As shown in the table, girls and boys are required to take four, mainly oral, tests, and ten practical exercises. Official statistics would indicate that most schools are successful in meeting these targets (that, for example, nine out of ten schoolchildren aged between twelve and seventeen pursued a sport regularly in 1970 and that almost one in four became proficient enough to gain a sports ranking). Other sources, however, tell a different story. In a survey carried out by *Komsomol'skaya pravda* among senior-form pupils in the city of Smolensk, it was found that only 232 out of 1,000 polled actually pursued a sport regularly. A speaker at the All-Union Conference on Physical Education, held in 1971, confirmed that "only a quarter of our children practise a sport regularly"; he blamed TV, the lack of sports-facilities and the hostile attitude of sports societies towards children.[37] Two years later, *Pravda* complained that only 20 per cent of schoolchildren regularly engaged in sport.[38]

All the same, schoolchildren evidently make a significant contribution to the country's sports-movement. They were said, in 1974, to make up 43 per cent of the country's regular sportsmen, over half the GTO badge-holders and a high proportion of ranked athletes. That sport features prominently in many children's out-of-school activities is apparent from a recent survey carried out in nine different cities. When asked how they spent their spare time, the respondents put sport in second place (in one town it came third) after reading and in front of watching TV, listening to music, going to the cinema and theatre, and collecting stamps, etc. When asked what they valued most from sport, the general consensus was health first, friendship second.[39]

It should be added that many schoolchildren engage in recreational activities through their Young Pioneer organisation (to which all Soviet children between nine and fifteen belong); moreover, many children spend at least a fortnight of their summer holiday in a camp, often under canvas in a forest or by the sea or a river. It was stated that

nearly one in three schoolchildren were in a Pioneer, school, sport or tourist camp during the summer of 1971 ... They all had a single objective: to establish a sports and health regime.[40]

According to an official statistical handbook, about one in four or five children were served by Pioneer camps in 1970.[41]

(ii) Physical education and sport among students

Unless excused by doctor's certificate, *all Soviet students must attend P.E. classes for the first two years of the (normally) five-year course.* If they do not attend enough P.E. classes and do not put up a satisfactory showing in the end-of-session test, they may be refused permission to continue their studies—irrespective of attendance and performance in academic subjects. Altogether, students must attend 140 hours of physical education during their first two years of study. After that, P.E. and games are voluntary. The physical education department is responsible for conducting the statutory P.E. lessons, but the student sports society, *Burevestnik*, is responsible for seeing that the planned percentage of students engage in sport and that a certain number of ranked students is produced every year.

(iii) Special sports schools

Young people who wish to pursue a sport seriously after school hours may do so in one of several specialised sports establishments that include a "children's and young people's sports school", a "sports proficiency school" and a "higher sports proficiency school". It is also possible to attend a full-time sports school from the age of seven that combines a normal school curriculum with sports training (like, for example, the football schools in Minsk and Moscow). If children show exceptional ability, they may even be admitted to full-time education and training in one of the special sports boarding schools.

(a) *Children's and young people's sports schools.* In 1977, there were 4,000 children's and young people's sports schools (CYPSS) with a total membership of a million and a half children.

Children are considered for a CYPSS on the recommendation of their school P.E. instructor or at the request of their parents. Attendance and coaching are free. Although most of the schools take children at eleven years of age, for some sports they may accept them earlier or later. For example, entrants to swimming-sections may be accepted at seven or eight although cyclists and speed-skaters can only be taken at thirteen or fourteen. How often they train depends on the sport and the school, but coaching is intensive and classes are often long and frequent. In the *Pervomaisky* District of Moscow, for instance, the CYPSS had, in 1974, preparatory groups of 11–13 years olds who had to attend three times a week for two-hour sessions in the evenings; each group had fifteen members. Some of the top groups did even more training: the youngsters working for their Master of Sport ranking had to attend four or five times a week for two-hour sessions. The Committee on Physical Culture and Sport laid down the conditions of work for all CYPSS's in a Statute on the schools published in February 1970. The programme for CYPSS's specialising in gymnastics gives some idea of how serious the training is taken. Thus, a fifteen-year-old boy or thirteen-year-old girl attending a school and working towards a First Ranking will be in a group of about six gymnasts, attending training sessions four times a week for three and a half to four hours each session (see Table 4). That is, by any standards, a considerable load in addition to school work. On a visit to the Spartak gymnastics school in Leningrad in the autumn of 1975, it was instructive to watch three young girl gymnasts in training (one was fourteen year-old Olga Koval, then a new member of the Soviet national team) with as many as four specialists in attendance: coaches in gymnastics and acrobatics, a choreographer and a conservatoire-trained pianist. They trained from ten to two each day, six days a week, and attended normal school in the afternoon—in the case of Olga Koval, this was the Leningrad Sports Boarding School. All instruction, facilities and equipment were, of course, free of charge.

Originally it was intended for these schools to cultivate up to ten sports, but most today concentrate on no more than three, some on only one sport. Their aim is to use the best of the limited facilities available in the USSR to give special coaching to young people in a

Table 4.   TRAINING CONDITIONS FOR A GYMNASTIC
CYPSS, 1970

Name of group	No. of groups	Age boys	Age girls	No. of pupils in the group	No. of sessions per week boys	No. of sessions per week girls	Length of each session (hours) boys	Length of each session (hours) girls
Preparatory	3	9	8	15	2	2	2	2
"Young Gymnast"	3	10	8–9	15	3	3	2	2
3rd Rank	3	12	11	12	3	4	3	2
2nd Rank	2	13	12	8	4	3	3	3
1st Rank	2	15	13	6	4	4	4	3·5
Candidate Master of Sport	1	17	14	4	5	5	4	3·5
Master of Sport	1	18	15	3–4	5	5	4	3·5

particular sport so that they may become proficient, gain a ranking and graduate to a national or a Republican team. They are one of the vital elements in Soviet sporting success, and are therefore provided with the best resources: of the 25,000 coaches working in the CYPSS's in 1967, some 80 per cent were qualified, compared with just over 55 per cent of P.E. instructors in secondary schools and 58 per cent of all full-time P.E. instructors and coaches in the country as a whole. Of the country's 42,310 full-time instructors and coaches in 1967, therefore, over half were working in the CYPSS's. It is also regarded as the duty of the country's top athletes that they should do some coaching and demonstrating in the schools regularly.

The organisations responsible for financing and running these schools are mainly the Republican education ministries, the trade-union sport societies and the big sports clubs run by Dinamo and the armed forces. Of the 2,772 CYPSS's that existed in 1967, the education ministries were responsible for 1,605 with an enrolment of 567,400 members, the trade-union societies for 1,044 with an enrolment of 296,000 and Dinamo and the armed forces for 123 with an enrolment of 74,700.

(b) *Sports boarding schools.* The USSR opened its first sports residential boarding-school in Tashkent in 1962—on the model of similar schools founded a few years earlier in East Germany. Soon afterwards, similar schools were created—at first, one in each of the fifteen Republics, then in some provincial centres. It was not until 1970, however, that a special government resolution was passed on their creation. By that time, about twenty already existed; another twenty-four were planned for the near future.

They follow other specialised boarding-schools (e.g. for cultivating mathematical, musical and artistic talents) in adhering to the standard curriculum for ordinary secondary schools, but having an additional specialised study-load in sports theory and practice. Their aim is for pupils to obtain the school-leaving certificate in addition to proficiency in a particular sport. Boarders are mostly accepted at eleven and stay on until the age of eighteen —a year longer than ordinary school.

Boys and girls are normally invited to the schools on the basis of performance in Republican school games. With the consent of their parents, they can enter the school if they pass an entrance examination and fairly stringent medical tests. Allocation of periods to sport in the timetable rises with each successive year of the course. For example, twelve-year-olds in the gymnastics section of the Tallinn school (which I visited in 1970) spent twenty-five hours per (six-day) week on standard subjects, plus eight hours on gymnastics, two on swimming and two on P.E. In the top form, at eighteen, they devoted twenty-three hours a week to sport, including nineteen hours of gymnastics. Roughly the same number of hours had to be spent on academic work. Despite this rigorous schedule, it is asserted that the pupils have a better-than-average health and academic record: the physical and mental aspects are said to supplement and reinforce one another. A gymnastics school in Dnepropetrovsk claims to show better academic results (as well as improved health and discipline) than ordinary day schools.

One reason for the founding of these schools is the realisation that early specialisation, especially in athletics, gymnastics and swimming, is essential to achieve high standards and hence success in international competition. It is no secret that the schools are expected to produce Olympic champions:

The sporting vocation has a particular significance not for mass sport, but for specialised sports-schools in such sports as athletics, swimming, gymnastics, team-games, figure-skating, skiing and speed-skating—i.e. in sports that constitute the basis of the Olympic programme. In evaluating the meaningfulness of sport in international tournaments, one must not forget that, while world and European championships have great importance, victory at the Olympic Games acquires a political resonance.[42]

The point made is that the Olympics carry more publicity and national prestige. They are regarded as *the* measure of a nation's health and power. And as many as 70 per cent of the Olympic medals are concentrated in three sports: athletics, swimming and gymnastics. The Soviet sports boarding schools, in fact, are concerned with Olympic sports *only*.

Despite some opposition to the schools, the future would seem to be with such centres of excellence. The official view regards talent in sport as precocious and, as in art, music and mathematics, requiring special nurturing to develop that talent to the full. It is therefore seen as sensible to bring together children of natural and instinctive aptitudes for sport in a "controlled" environment of a residential school, served by the best coaches and amenities, nurtured on a special diet, constantly supervised by sports instructors and doctors, and stimulated by mutual interest and enthusiasm.

III. *Professional training*

One of the requirements for active athletes is that, at the same time as they train and engage in competition at home and abroad, they should improve their theoretical knowledge by studying. In fact, a large proportion of leading Soviet athletes, mostly Masters, are provided with the relative security of a studentship or postgraduate scholarship at one of the country's institutes of physical culture. A number of top-flight sportsmen spend as much as ten or fifteen years at these educational establishments—as long, in fact, as they remain active and successful in their sport. This is, of course, a system of "sports scholarships" not uncommon in the USA. It would seem, however, that for many Soviet Masters, academic work is an integral and important part of their training and is taken seriously.[43] It is felt that this is one way of preparing a sportsman for a future career once his short-lived active participation is over.[44]

Apart from part-time student sportsmen, the secondary and higher education establishments teach a large number of students who become instructors, coaches and officials in schools, colleges, sports-societies, clubs, factories and farms. The range of physical-education teaching and research establishments is as follows:

Table 5.   PHYSICAL EDUCATION ESTABLISHMENTS 1972

Type of Educational Establishment	Number
1. Institutes of physical culture (*instituty fizkul'tury*)	20
2. Physical-education faculties at higher education establishments (*fakul'tety fizicheskovo vospitaniya*)	78
3. Secondary special physical-culture education establishments (*tekhnikumy fizkul'tury*)	25
4. Secondary special colleges of education specialising in physical education (*pedagogicheskie uchilischcha fizkul'turnovo profilya*)	33
5. Schools for coaches attached to physical-culture institutes or secondary special education establishments (*shkoly trenerov pri institutakh, tekhnikumakh fizicheskoi kul'tury*)	18
6. Physical-culture research institutes (*nauchnoissledovatel'-skie instituty fizkul'tury*)	4

Students for the institutes of physical culture are normally accepted for one of two degree-courses: Education or Sport. In the former, on graduation after a four-year course, students become teachers of physical education with the right to work in schools and colleges, sports societies or urban and rural sports collectives. In the latter, graduates receive the qualification of "Instructor-Coach" with the right to work as coach in any sports organisation.

The physical education faculties train students to become P.E. in-structors in secondary schools after a four-year course which closely parallels the Education curricula of the institutes of physical culture.

The physical-culture colleges (*tekhnikums*) also train P.E. instructors for schools and coaches in individual sports for urban and rural sports collectives. Most of the entrants are accepted at the age of fifteen or sixteen straight from general school and undergo a course of between four and five years; evening and correspondence-course students do an extra year.

The secondary special colleges of education specialising in physical education fulfil more or less the same function as the tekhnikums in training P.E. instructors for secondary schools. The study-course is shorter (usually three years) and the teaching less intensive. Normally, entrants are taken at the age of fifteen having completed eight years of general education.

Schools for coaches are normally attached either to an institute of physical culture or to a tekhnikum. Although they do take students at the age of fifteen or sixteen from secondary school, they are chiefly concerned with evening and correspondence courses for experienced sportsmen who wish to gain a coaching certificate during their sports career. Courses last approximately four years for internal students plus an extra year for external students.

It should be pointed out that most P.E. qualifications, like higher degrees generally, are obtained by means of correspondence and evening courses. Entry is therefore far more open to such courses than it is in many other countries; it is also more possible—indeed, there is great encouragement—for workers or men and women of mature years, especially ex-athletes, to obtain such a diploma or degree. The recently-retired gymnast, Ludmilla Turishcheva, for example, having obtained her coaching diploma while still an active sportswoman, moved directly into coaching upon retirement, combining this with a doctoral dissertation on "Effects of Pre-Performance Emotional Tension in Gymnastics on Competitive Performance". This is by no means uncommon.

Research into physical education and sport is an integral part of the Soviet sports-movement. It is conducted at a large number of higher-education establishments, including all the institutes of physical culture and the physical-education faculties, at medical colleges, polytechnics, at the Academy of Medical Sciences of the USSR and, most important of all, at one of the latter's institutes (the Research Institute of Physiology and Physical Education) and at three separate, physical-culture research-institutes. A special library of books, periodicals and films concerned exclusively with sport and physical education is situated in Minsk, capital of Byelorussia.

As may be gathered from the description above of the various educational courses, a scientific and technological study of sport and its related sciences is regarded as vital to a real understanding of the significance of sport in everyday life and work, and the basis for improved performance. Such subjects as biomechanics, cybernetics and electronics may be considered as part of the Russian and Soviet concern with the technical side of physical education and are a continuation of the tradition of such Russian scientists as Sechyonov, Pavlov and Lesgaft. In the early 1970s, research was also being pursued into the sociology of sport—an area hitherto largely unexplored in the Soviet Union and still circumscribed by rather narrow ideological boundaries.

IV. *Sport in Soviet society: some general conclusions*

1. While not wishing to overstate the importance of sport in Soviet society, it seems reasonable to assume that sport has had particular social significance in Soviet development. All the more so because it is evidently more central in the Soviet system. In a vast multinational land that has witnessed disorientingly rapid change, sport has extended to and united wider sections of the population than probably any other social activity. It has proved to be of peculiar utility by reason of its inherent qualities of being easily understood and enjoyed, being apolitical (at least superficially) and permitting emotional release safely. It has thus had an advantage over drinking, sex, religious ritual and other forms of emotional release and companionship-formation by being officially approved and therefore less guilt-inducing, and yet being relatively free of rigid official sanctions. It has had an advantage over literature, theatre and other forms of cultural expression by being more readily comprehensible to the mass public as well as less amenable to direct political control over style and content.

These advantages have been particularly marked in a society which has, in a short span of time, lived through such shattering events as two world wars, three revolutions, a civil war, rapid industrialisation, forced collectivisation, purges and mass terror. In this society, hard work, discipline, self-censorship and periodically necessary acute re-adjustments may well have needed a counterpart in sport, offering as it does a particularly rewarding area of relaxation and recreation.

2. In the development of Soviet society, sport has always been state-controlled, encouraged and shaped by specific utilitarian and ideological designs—primarily for labour and military training and the all-round development of the ideal citizen. Sport was proclaimed an essential part of the way of life of *all* citizens. This state-centralised control of sport has prevented commercial exploitation of mass spectator sports for private profit and the playing of particular sports in which actual or simulated violence predominated, and has inhibited the extremes of hooliganism, corruption and commercialism associated with a number of sports in the West.

3. In practical policy, the Soviet leaders, from about 1928 on, would seem to have opted for the following in developing forms of recreation: (i) cultivating competitive sport (a leisure-time analogue of the competition between people at work designed to raise work-tempos)

with—again, as at work—material rewards for victors, the more effectively to improve people's readiness for work and to pre-train soldiers for the Soviet nation-state;

(ii) using sport, specifically, as a means of obtaining the fit, obedient and disciplined work-force needed for achieving economic and military strength and efficiency—in particular in order

(a) to raise physical and social health-standards—and the latter meant not simply educating people in the virtues of bodily hygiene, regular exercise and sound nutrition, but also overcoming unhealthy deviant, anti-social (and therefore anti-Soviet) behaviour: drunkenness, delinquency, prostitution—even religiosity and intellectual dissidence;

(b) to socialise the population into the new establishment system of values; character-training, advanced (so the Soviet leaders seem to have believed) by sport, in such values as loyalty, conformity, team-spirit, cooperation and discipline, may well have encouraged compliance and cooperation in both work and politics;

(c) to encourage a population, in transition from a rural to an urban way of life, to identify themselves with wider communities—all-embracing social units such as the workplace, the neighbourhood, the town, the district, the republic and ultimately, the whole country. By associating sport (like other amenities) organisationally with the workplace, the Party leadership and its agencies could, moreover, better supervise and "rationalise" the leisure-time activities of employees;

(iii) linking sport ideologically and even organisationally with military preparedness; the reasons for this "militarisation" of sport must be sought in:

(a) the leadership's fear of war and its conviction of the need to keep the population primed to meet it;

(b) the all-pervasive presence throughout society of the military and security forces, necessitated by the imposition from above, should enthusiasm from below flag, of "socialist construction" on a tired public (a state of affairs not so odd-seeming in Russian society, since this military presence had also, if for different reasons, been the norm before the revolution, in sport as elsewhere);

(c) the fact that, in a vast country with problems of communication, lukewarm (at best) popular attitudes towards physical exercise and few sports facilities for most of the Soviet period, military organisation of sport was actually an efficient method of deploying scarce resources in the most economical way and using methods of direction which were, perhaps, more effective coming from paramilitary than from civilian organisations.

Given all that has been said, it would seem logical that sport could not have been allowed to develop haphazardly in the USSR, in the hands of individual enthusiasts who could make the playing of their sport exclusive to a particular social group, class sex or race—as had happened in Anglo-Saxon countries particularly. Sport is regarded as being far too important for that. It is seen as vital for the all-round development of the individual and ultimately for the health of the community. More than that: it has been used quite consciously by Soviet leaders as a means to change society.

NOTES

1. M. Lewin, *Lenin's Last Struggle*, London, 1975, p. 12.
2. N. I. Podvoisky, *O militsionnoi organizatsii vooruzhennykh sil Rossiyskoi Sovetskoi Federativnoi Sotsialisticheskoi Republiki*, Moscow, 1923, p. 9.
3. Ibid, p. 41.
4. For information on this remarkable festival see *Izvestiya* Tashkent, No. 232, p. 1; *K novoi Armii*, 1920, No. 19-20, pp. 18-19.
5. *Sport* v. *SSSR*, 1973, No. 5, p. 9.
6. The Proletkult (abbreviation for "Proletarian Cultural and Educational Organisation") was formed in 1917 with the intention of producing a proletarian culture as an indispensible part of a socialist revolution, and rejecting all previous culture as a product of class society. It became widely influential but was eventually abolished in 1932.
7. M. A. Kornilieva-Radina, Ya. P. Radin, *Novym detyam—novye igry*, Moscow, 1927, p. 37.
8. *Izvestiya tsentral'novo komiteta RKP(b)*, 20 July 1925.
9. Ibid.
10. *Teoriya i praktika fizicheskoi kul'tury*, 1972, No. 12, p. 13.
11. Ibid.
12. *Fizkul'tura i sport*, 1970, No. 6, p. 5.
13. Ibid.
14. *Pravda*, 22 June 1922.
15. It has been calculated that a shift of labour comparable to that which took place in the USSR in the twelve years between 1928 and 1940 had taken from thirty to fifty years in the countries of Western Europe and North America that had industrialised earlier (see C. E. Black, "Soviet Society: A Comparative View", ed. A. Kassof, *Prospects for Soviet Society*, New York, 1968, p. 32). Moscow, for example, increased in population from just over one million in 1920 to over two million in 1926, nearly three million in 1931 and over four million in 1939 (*Moskva arkhitekturny putevoditel'*, Moscow, 1960, p. 6).
16. In 1926, the average housing space per person had only been 8·2 and, by 1940, it was down to 6·4 square metres. (*Narodnoye khozyaistvo SSSR v 1970*, Moscow, 1971, p. 7, 546.)
17. Although virtually no mention of the fact is now made in Soviet publications, Dinamo still today "is under the control of the USSR Ministry of Internal Affairs and the Committee on State Security (KGB) attached to the

USSR Council of Ministers". See M. F. Bunchuk, *Organizatsiya fizicheskoi kul'tury*, Moscow, 1972, p. 81.

18. G. D. Kharabuga, *Sovetskaya sistema fizicheskovo vospitaniya*, Leningrad, 1970, p. 13.

19. See *Pravda*, 22 October 1945, p. 1.

20. See I. D. Chudinov, *Osnovnye postanovleniya, prikazy i instruktsii po voprosam fizicheskoi kul'tury i sporta, 1917–1957*, Moscow, 1950, p. 189.

21. See *Kul'tura i zhizn'*, 11 January 1949, p. 3.

22. The IOC continued to recognise the old tsarist Russian Olympic Committee for several years after 1917. Such ROC members as General Butovsky, Count Ribopierre, Baron Vilebrandt and Prince Urusov all served on the IOC in the period 1917–32.

23. A. O. Romanov, *Mezhdunarodnoye sportivnoye dvizhenie*, Moscow, 1973, p. 193.

24. Soviet statistics indicate that as many as 40 million people took part in the Second Spartakiad in 1959, 66 million in the Third, between 57 and 80 million in the Fourth, 44 million in the Fifth and 80 million in the Sixth in 1975 (i.e. a third of the population). See *Sport v SSSR*, 1975, No. 10, p. 9.

25. It is estimated that, by 1980–5, the USSR will have some 15–20 million passenger cars—i.e. approximately one for every four to five families. (See L. A. Gordon, E. V. Klopov, *Chelovek posle raboty*, Moscow, 1972, p. 273).

26. For example, motor racing and rallying, yachting, karting, various winter sports (tobogganing, bobsleighing, slaloming, ski-jumping), water-skiing, aqua-lung diving, mountain-climbing, fishing and shooting, and the complex of activities that come under the rubric of "tourism" all showed appreciable growth in the 1960s. Some sports received a new lease of life as industry was able to produce equipment for them—as, for example, in the cases of rugby, archery and field hockey. The most recently-introduced sports for which facilities are at present being constructed are squash and hanggliding. Some republics increased their expenditure on sports facilities by as much as six or seven times after 1966.

27. In 1956, the standard (six-day) week in Soviet industry was of 46 hours; by 1961, it had declined to 41 hours—still in a six-day week—i.e. most workers had five seven-hour days and one six-hour day each week. In 1970, the average working week in industry was 40·7 hours and, in state employment in general, 39·4 hours in a five-day week. The number of public holidays and days off for industrial manual workers increased by 36·1 days between 1960 and 1972; time actually worked declined by 33.9 days in the same period. Altogether, Soviet industrial manual workers had 95·4 days off during 1974, including annual paid holidays of 15 days for most workers.

28. Whereas only 18 per cent of the Soviet population lived in towns in 1926, today 60 per cent is urban-based—i.e. three fifths of a population exceeding a quarter of a billion. Furthermore, the USSR has eleven cities with a population exceeding one million, thirty-five cities with a population of over half a million. See *SSSR v. tsifrakh v 1973 godu*, Moscow, 1971, pp. 7, 13, 14, 17.

29. See L. A. Gordon, N. M. Rimashevskaya, *Pyatidnevnaya rabochaya nedelya i svobodnoye vremya trudyashchikhsya*, Moscow, 1972, pp. 38–9.

30. *Teoriya i praktika fizicheskoi kul'tury*, 1973, No. 10, p. 62.

31. *Sovetsky sport*, 25 January 1973, p. 3.
32. *Teoriya i praktika fizicheskoi kul'tury*, 1973, No. 10, p. 61.
33. Ibid, p. 64.
34. *Pravda*, 25 August 1966, p. 2.
35. V. S. Kayurov (ed.), *Kniga uchitelya fizicheskoi kul'tury*, Moscow, 1973, p. 11.
36. *Fizkul'tura i sport*, 1975, No. 9, p. 3.
37. *Sovetsky sport*, 17 December 1971. p. 3.
38. *Pravda*, 5 August 1973, p. 2.
39. *Teoriya i praktika fizicheskoi kul'tury*, 1972, No. 4, p. 35.
40. *Sovetsky sport*, 1 July 1971, p. 2.
41. *Narodnoye khozyaistvo SSSR v 1970 g.* (Moscow, 1971), pp. 633, 636.
42. *Teoriya i praktika fizicheskoi kul'tury*, 1968, No. 5, p. 42. For more information, see my article "Sports Boarding Schools in the USSR", in *Journal of Physical Education and Recreation*, May 1975, pp. 7–8.
43. In early 1971, I accompanied a Soviet friend (who was then an international footballer) to the Central State Institute of Physical Culture in Moscow —his alma mater. During the tour of the institute, it became quite evident that he had actually studied there for five years. He also said that nobody is permitted to play in league football without completing ten years of schooling. Moreover, of the twenty-seven footballers attached to the permament staff of Moscow Spartak, twenty-four were studying or had studied in a higher educational establishment. On our way out of the institute, we met a group of footballers (from three other Moscow clubs) who were just arriving for evening classes.
44. Among Soviet boxers, for example—a sporting profession by repute not generally noted in the West for the high intelligence of its practitioners— former USSR champion, Konstantin Gradopol, is now a university professor, former Olympic champion, Gennady Shatkov, is rector of Leningrad University, one former Olympic champion, Boris Lagutin, is now a practising barrister and another, Valery Popenchenko (holder of the Barker Trophy as best boxer at the 1964 Olympic Games), was awarded in 1968 a Ph.D (*kandidat tekhnicheskikh nauk*) for his research.

Vladimir Kostka

CZECHOSLOVAKIA

PERSONAL NOTE

Dr. Kostka is Dean of the Faculty of Physical Education and Sport at Charles University, Prague, and a member of the Senate of Charles University. In addition, he is Chairman of the Specialist Committee on Physical Education and Sport attached to the Education Ministry and member of the Scientific Board of the Czechoslovak Physical Education Association. His long-time involvement in ice hockey included being coach to the Czechoslovak national team for eleven years, during which time it won the world championship once and the European championship three times. Dr. Kostka is a Merited Coach and member of the Coaches' Committee of the International Ice Hockey Federation. His many publications include *Modern Ice Hockey* and *Attack in Ice Hockey*; these and others have been translated and published in Canada, Finland, the GDR, Japan, Rumania, the USSR and Sweden.

CONTENTS

Introduction

The Czechoslovak Socialist Republic is a Central European country, small in physical size and population.[1] It is, however, a land rich in tradition which has been carefully preserved in all cultural areas, including physical culture. Czechoslovak physical culture therefore draws on national traditions enriched by modern theory and practice. Characteristically, the concept of socialist physical culture has always been linked, in our country, with a social commitment and a readiness to embrace the best ideas of social progress.

I. *Socialist physical culture*

Physical culture in Czechoslovakia is centrally planned and organised; here lies the source of its success in international competition: at the Olympics, world and European championships.

It is a constituent part of the socialist education system and is therefore actively supported by the government and all public organisations. Further, it is integrated into a popular system of upbringing of the younger generation which embodies the ideas of the great Czech educational reformer, Jan Komenský,[2] notably his insistence that all human beings should be educated in a systematic way from birth to late old age. This concept of "permanent education" fully applies to Czechoslovak physical culture, incorporating as it does a wide range of physical activity:

1. compulsory (at school and college; in the armed forces);
2. voluntary (based on the national sports programme elaborated by the Czechoslovak Sports Union);
3. organised recreation that comes within the purview of such organisations as the Socialist Youth League[3] and the trade unions;
4. individual or family recreation.

The Czechoslovak Sports Union is organisationally associated with the National Front which is of particular significance in Czechoslovak life, inasmuch as it is a coalition of all political parties, the trade unions, the Socialist Youth League and cultural associations under the leadership of the Communist Party of Czechoslovakia. It is through this coalition that the Sports Union has its own representatives at all levels of administration, and can thereby influence sports provision directly at local and national levels; it has legislative powers right up to the supreme legislative body of the country.

II. *Origins and development of sport in Czechoslovakia*

Sport has played an important rôle in the history of the Czech and Slovak nations. This was especially so after 1862 when the first gymnastics association, the Prague Sokol, came into being. From its centre in Prague, the Sokol ("Falcon") movement spread throughout the land and did much to bring about a national renaissance. This first Czech gymnastics organisation did not confine itself to physical education; from the outset the idea of physical fitness was linked with political aims—primarily the struggle for national independence against Austro-Hungarian cultural and political repression. The founder of Sokol, Dr. Miroslav Tyrš (1832–84), gave the movement explicitly ideological and practical aims. His progressive and noble ideals of patriotism, democracy and Slavdom enhanced the authority of the Sokol movement among the people. Sokol gymnastics were based on the all-round development of participants and included all forms of gymnastic activity. Moreover, from 1869 women were permitted to take part in the Sokol programme, and this made an important contribution to their fight for emancipation during the 1870s. The Sokol programme provided for a uniform set of exercises and activities basically similar to the sports programme existing in Czechoslovakia today. Gymnasts employed such apparatus as the parallel bars, the horse and the beam, engaged in athletics, fencing and wrestling, and mass drill, the last as an expression of the nation's defensive capabilities. To this was added, in women's Sokol gymnastics during the 1880s, a free and artistic combination of exercises performed to music, giving stress to graceful movement and an elaboration of various exercises for different age groups. Mass gymnastics for pre-school children performed on a parade ground or field was introduced, as were various exercises in group therapeutic gymnastics.

An important coordinating feature of this system was that the compulsory and voluntary engagement in sport and physical education was supervised by the same people: school physical education was taught by persons who were also Sokol instructors. This coordinating function led to a coherence in the content and teaching methods of school and college physical education, and therefore to a uniform basis for both compulsory and voluntary physical culture. Insistence on high standards of teacher-training further enhanced the reputation of physical education and facilitated the application of a uniform system.

The Sokol movement had its own journal and literature from its very inception; this helped to ensure ideological and professional unity. The political circumstances were such that the Czech bourgeoisie was becoming increasingly influential; and this encouraged a uniformity within the Sokol movement. Furthermore, a mounting class-consciousness among the industrial workers was evident within the sports associations. After the rupture with the Social Democrats, the first working-class sports association came into being in 1897. From that point on, the growing divergence in political aims within the sports movement made itself increasingly felt. Other sports organisations were formed, often basing themselves on much of the Sokol's work, even though their own ideological objectives were different. In 1921, when the Communist Party of Czechoslovakia was founded, it brought into being a revolutionary working-class sports organisation: the Federation of Workers' Sports Associations, later to be known as the Proletarian Sports Federation. It brought together working men and women and laid the foundation for the revolutionary traditions that are an integral part of socialist physical culture today.

During the nineteenth century, other organised sports took a hold in Czechoslovakia. Amongst the oldest are athletics, cycling, rowing, skating and tennis. After 1896, when the Czech Olympic Committee was founded, sporting traditions became linked with the development of the Olympic Games. Some competitions that date from this period have survived until today. For example, a road-race championship *Běchovice* has been run over the same course since 1897; the first eights rowing race, the *Primátorky*, was held in 1910 and has become an annual fixture. Czech handball had its initial competition in 1905. In field events, the famous discus-thrower, František Janda-Suk, is still remembered for his innovatory technique in the turn. Sokol gymnasts won many international victories in apparatus gymnastics.

Sport continued to have essentially the same organisational structure during the bourgeois republic of 1918–38. During this period of growing class conflict, the sports movement became splintered into a number of organisations, corresponding to the political structure of the state. Joint activities took place only when the republic was threatened, when most sports bodies were brought together in defence of their country against Nazi Germany.

Until World War II, then, the following progress had been made: (a) the most important popular achievements were the widespread sports festivals: the Sokol festivals, the working-class Olympics, and the Spartakiadas of the revolutionary workers' sports movement. The last-named included the 1936 People's Games held in Prague, which demonstrated international solidarity for peace and against fascism; (b) the most successful individual sports were gymnastics, rowing, weightlifting, wrestling, women's athletics, table-tennis, football, ice-hockey and archery. In all these sports, the country gained Olympic medals and top places in world or European championships.

Sport was suppressed during the war: the largest sports organisations were proscribed and many sports officials and even ordinary members were imprisoned and executed. However, with the defeat of fascism in 1945, it was once again possible to promote sport which, in line with government policy, came under a central organisation. But it was not until February 1948, when Czechoslovakia took the socialist path of development, that the entire sports movement was unified. The new national sports organisation soon became a paramount part of the social life of Czechoslovakia. The structure of the sports movement had now altered; no longer was it divided, as it had been under the bourgeois republic. Its guiding principles and ideals brought it more into line with the newly formed sports systems in the other socialist states and the USSR. Nonetheless, the national character of Czechoslovak sport and physical education was fully retained as an expression of Czechoslovak national culture.

At the present stage of socialist physical culture, this gradual development has moved into a stable period that corresponds to the contemporary conditions prevailing in the country.

III. *Physical culture today*

(i) *In school and colleges*

Compulsory physical education comes within the competence of the appropriate government ministries, of which the most relevant to schools and colleges is the Ministry of Education. The latter's responsibilities apply to the following levels of education: 1. nursery schools; 2. general secondary schools; 3. trade schools; 4. special schools (for children in need of special care), and 5. colleges and universities.

All schools and colleges have a minimum of two lessons of compulsory physical education each week. Additionally, for those young people who display a special talent in sport, there are special classes in the Olympic sports, with an extended teaching programme in physical education. The P.E. syllabus is laid down for all schools and colleges by the Ministry in special manuals. Besides the P.E. lessons, games afternoons exist at schools on a non-compulsory basis. For children with impaired health, special P.E. departments operate with regard to the nature of the particular impairment.

In nursery schools (3–6 years old), physical education is part of the everyday curriculum and related to basic training in health and hygiene. It includes morning exercises, walks and outings, and free-play activity to which trained physical educationalists contribute twice a week.

At the first stage of compulsory schooling (6–11 year olds), the physical education programme is intended to encourage the all-round development of pupils. It focuses on natural exercises, competitive games, rhythmical and deportment exercises; the P.E. syllabus is backed up by recreational activity in the school sports clubs.

At the second stage (12–15 year olds), sports training is an integral part of the P.E. syllabus. In addition, we emphasise acrobatics, special exercises to develop good posture and general gymnastics. Apart from these lessons, there are sports clubs for those enthusiasts who wish to pursue a sport out of school time.

At the third stage (ages 16–19), the general approach to physical culture becomes more specialised, while spreading the range of individual sports activity. As before, the compulsory lessons are supplemented by optional participation in the school sports clubs.

Young people of school age are classified in groups according to their somatic type, for which national indices of performance exist—as a means of evaluating the effectiveness of the overall programme of physical education.

At colleges and universities, physical education is compulsory for all students: two hours per week during the first two years of their course, and one hour per week during the next two years; in addition to this they may pursue sports of their choice.

(ii) Sport for the general public

Provision for sport and recreation in the country at large comes mainly under the Czechoslovak Sports Union. In 1948, all former sports and tourist organisations banded together to form this Union. On 1 January 1976, it had as many as 1,636,000 members, of which 956,000 were adults, 230,000 were young people at work or studying, and 450,000 were schoolchildren. Of the total, 445,000 were females.

The Sports Union is a public organisation whose principal task is to facilitate the all-round development of all citizens. It has government backing and is run on democratic centralist lines—i.e. it is guided by its Central Council through the governing bodies of the country's two republics, the Czech and the Slovak, down through the regions and districts to the primary sports associations in the localities. Its main responsibilities consist in the following:
1. to encourage regular and active participation in sport for everyone, above all through the Federation of Physical Fitness and Recreation (over 430,000 members) and the Tourist Association (over 100,000 members); and 2. to ensure the effectiveness of top-level sport within the forty-three sports federations, which have in excess of 1,100,000 members.

The figures given above for overall participation are actually greater if we include all persons who take part in some form of active recreation in other institutions concerned with sport. Thus, more than 100,000 people compete annually in sports tournaments specifically for apprentices; some 65,000 participate in annual rural sports tourneys; some 150,000 ramblers regularly engage in long-distance walks, and so on. In 1975, over 253,000 Czechoslovaks competed for the national fitness badge "Ready for Labour and Defence of the Homeland". The single most important event in the "sport for all" campaign is the Czechoslovak Spartakiada. This is a festival of physical culture which is associated with the progressive traditions of the Sokol festivals and the workers' Spartakiadas. Today, the Spartakiada includes a wide range of sports and outdoor recreational activities. The focal point of the festival, however, is to involve ordinary men, women and children in sport at some stage between the local preliminaries and the Finals, held in the Strahov Stadium in Prague. During the 1975 Spartakiada, 180,000 athletes took part in the Prague Finals watched by 728,000 spectators. As many as 1,529,000 participants and 2,961,000 spectators were involved in the local and district Spartakiadas.

It is a rule that the Spartakiadas should be associated with anniversaries commemorating the national liberation struggle and Czechoslovakia's liberation by the Soviet Army in the last war. The centrepiece of the festival is an artistic excercise display, featuring graceful movement and choreographed configurations, thereby symbolically expressing popular aspirations in physical culture. During the festival in the Strahov Stadium, 15,000 performers can be accommodated at one time in the central arena (measuring 300m. by 200m.). These Spartakiadas also bear a political significance, in so far as they are simultaneously a spontaneous manifestation of the political unity of our nation and peoples.

IV. *Federation of physical fitness and recreation*

The traditional Czechoslovak conception of physical culture, enriched by contemporary knowledge, is the basis of the work of this Federation Its programme of activities consists of a whole range of interrelated pursuits for members of all ages. The first link in this chain of lifetime physical culture is a set of gymnastics exercises for parents together with their children (from three years and upwards); the last link is a set of exercises for the aged. Besides basic gymnastics groups, the Federation organises keep-fit classes, calisthenics and modern rhythmic gymnastics groups, plus a wide range of indoor and outdoor recreational activities and competitive sports. It publishes programmes of exercises and qualifying standards for all these groups; these provide guidelines and targets to aim at. The foundation of all such activities is regular exercise supplemented by the attraction of mass competitions and displays. Women play a particularly important part in the latter, since they comprise a majority of the Federation's members.

This widespread sports participation is made possible primarily by the selfless dedication of more than 28,000 voluntary coaches and instructors who give their services free of charge. Branches of the Federation operate in most parts of the country and constitute the main channel through which all citizens in town and country are drawn into regular and active sport and recreation.

V. *Tourist association*

This is a national organisation concerned with involving the public in regular outdoor recreation. In recent years, it has had a great influx of members, especially young people. It is responsible for a whole range of activities that fall under the general rubric of outdoor recreation: from rambling to rock-climbing, from long-distance hikes to pot-holing.

VI. *Sports federations*

Individual competitive sports come under the aegis of the sports federations whose function it is both to involve people in regular sporting pursuits and to prepare individual athletes and teams for top-class competition. All the federations have a uniform organisational structure and training system. This coordinated structure and approach enable them to operate a joint programme of training and competition from the lowest to the topmost levels of performance. More than 65,000 voluntary coaches take part in implementing these programmes.

Apart from the regular training sessions for proficient athletes, the federations are responsible for centrally-planned competition at all levels, from local tournaments right up to national leagues, cups and championships. Talented athletes who represent their country internationally are provided with special training facilities in so-called centres of excellence run by full-time coaches and officials. Public interest in top sports performance and international events is apparent in the large crowds that the big sports competitions draw. Some sports are especially popular and may be regarded as national sports—such as football and ice-hockey, in both of which Czechoslovakia has gained considerable international success over the years. In 1975, Czechoslovakia provided the European football champions and the world ice-hockey champions.

In the thirty years from 1945 to 1975, Czechoslovakia achieved substantial international success in sport. It gained, for example, a total of thirty-three gold, twenty-seven silver and twenty-three bronze Olympic medals. Among its world renowned stars are Emil Zatopek, Ludvik Danek, Dana Zatopkova, and the women's gymnastics team led by Eva Bosakova and Vera Caslavska. The boxers Julius Torms, Jan Zachara and Bohumil Nemecek also gained a lasting reputation in their sport. Czechoslovakia has also a good record in such sports as rowing, canoeing, ski-jumping and figure-skating: the first Czechoslovak gold medals at a Winter Olympics were won by Jiri Raska in ski-jumping and Ondrej Nepela in figure-skating.

In this thirty-year period, Czechoslovak athletes have gained: 147 firsts, 202 seconds and 215 thirds in world championships; 81 firsts, 107 seconds and 187 thirds in European championships. Altogether, Czechoslovak sportsmen and women have won world titles in fifteen separate sports and European titles in sixteen sports.

VII. *Public recognition for service to sport*

Socialist society values highly the work of people who dedicate themselves to sport and physical education. The supreme sporting accolade, the title of "Merited Worker in Physical Culture", is awarded personally by the President of the Republic and, jointly with another high honour, bears the names of the founder of Czechoslovak physical culture, Miroslav Tyrš and the founder of worker sport in Czechoslovakia, Jiri František Chaloupecký. Outstanding coaches and instructors are awarded the titles of "Merited Coach" and "Merited Instructor", and "Model Coach" and "Model Instructor". First, second and third degree awards are granted for long-standing service to sport. Excellence in sport is recognised by the titles "Merited Master of Sport" and "Master of Sport". Apart from these sporting awards, the government and Communist Party bestow the supreme state honours and titles upon the most esteemed of the country's sportsmen, coaches and officials.

VIII. *Sports personnel*

The extent and quality of performance and of international success in sport mainly depend on the work of both professional and part-time sports personnel. Typically in Czechoslovakia, most of this work is in the hands of part-timers involved in coaching and administration. All such personnel must attend nationally-organised courses which are run and supported by the individual sports organisations. These courses are all free of charge and are designed to improve the qualifications of their participants. In the event of an extended course that would normally interfere with a participant's full-time job, the person concerned may obtain paid leave of absence from his place of employment. The work of coaches and instructors is considered work for the public benefit and therefore receives generous financial support from the authorities. The Czechoslovak Sports Union has its own publishing house which issues manuals, magazines and newsletters for all sports personnel.

The college training of specialists in sport and physical education is becoming increasingly vital in order to meet today's high standards and requirements. This training is done primarily in the faculties of physical education and sport at Charles University in Prague and at the Komenský University in Bratislava. These faculties prepare teachers of physical education for secondary schools and specialists who will eventually work in the state sports agencies, as coaches or administrators in the various sports federations, as academics and researchers in such institutions as the Academy of Science. The full-time undergraduate courses run for five years, but graduates have to take a refresher course after five years of employment. In addition to the normal degrees in physical education, both faculties (at Charles and Komenský universities) award the degrees Doctor of Philosophy and Doctor of Natural Sciences to successful research students who have completed oral and written examinations and a satisfactory thesis. The supreme academic award in physical education is Candidate of Pedagogical Science, obtained by way of an outstanding scholarly dissertation. Concern for the quality of teacher-training in physical education has led in recent years to the introduction of higher-educational courses for primary school teachers. These courses are offered by educational departments in the various regions of the country.

A large sum of money is necessarily involved in training specialists at universities, in organising provision for sport, in constructing amenities and in manufacturing sports equipment, in ensuring the efficient functioning of the sports federations and the successful performance of Czechoslovak athletes in international sport. These funds come mainly from the government budget, the financial resources of factories, offices and farms, and from such sources available to sports organisations (as "gate receipts", etc.). Minor sporting facilities are provided through voluntary public work which often represents a financial saving of millions of crowns. This latter is a unique contribution by ordinary men and women for the good of sport.

IX. *Place of physical culture in society*

The entire activity of the Czechoslovak sports movement is aimed at preparing citizens for work and defence. These legally-enacted and supported aims are implemented through the medium of physical culture, in which elements of education and recreation form a dialectical unity. This high regard and concern for active involvement in physical culture for all ages and walks of life fully accord with the needs of the community. It is in the interests of society that full provision be made for health, fitness and recreation.

The interests of health mean improving the physical fitness of the population, enhancing people's capacity for work, and ensuring that they remain physically active in later years. Physical exercise is here reinforced by the health service which protects the health of all sports participants and, in case of injury, ensures their treatment and rehabilitation free of charge.

In regard to physical and mental fitness, sport has a part to play within the entire framework of socialist education, to which all public organisations, workplaces and families contribute. The foundation of this fitness is systematic educational work within the group, team or collective in which the individual personality is shaped, in which his interpersonal relations are established, and in which he develops a sense of belonging to the specific group or, in this case, sports collective; this ultimately grows into a higher sense of socialist patriotism and even internationalism. The ultimate goal of such education is to promote the moral outlook and other values of all citizens in the country and to instil a political awareness.

The formal aspects of recreation are provided for in the programme of activities organised by the individual sports federations, in the consistent application of a uniform system (based on common aims and central planning), and in respect of individual differences in age and interest among children and adults.

Physical culture is an integral part of the entire cultural life of present-day Czechoslovakia; it is therefore subject to social development. The overall policy on physical culture is given shape by the five-year plans drawn up for the whole of Czechoslovak society. Future trends and policies in sport must consequently be in harmony with the country's economic and social development. The concern for sport shown by state bodies, the government and the Communist Party assures the future of Czechoslovak physical culture as an integral part of society.

NOTES

1. Czechoslovakia has a population of some 15 million and an area of nearly 50,000 sq. miles—about the same size as Greece. It was created out of the dual monarchy of Austria–Hungary in 1918 from the old Slav kingdoms of Bohemia, Moravia, Slovakia and Ruthenia. It became a socialist republic in 1948. Today 68 per cent of the population is Czech and 28 per cent Slovak.

2. Jan Amos Komenský (Comenius), 1625–70.

3. Youth organisation open to young people between the ages 15–25, similar to the *Komsomol* in the USSR.

David Childs

THE GERMAN
DEMOCRATIC REPUBLIC

PERSONAL NOTE

Dr. Childs is Reader in Politics at Nottingham University, England. Educated at London and Hamburg Universities, he was awarded his doctorate for a thesis on the German Social Democratic Party. He has visited the GDR regularly since 1951 and has extensive contacts there. His book *East Germany* has been described as "an indispensable work of reference" (*Times Literary Supplement*); Dr. Childs' other books are *Marx and the Marxists, Germany Since 1918* and *From Schumacher to Brandt*.

CONTENTS

Introduction

Not very much is known about the German Democratic Republic (GDR) even among the educated segment of the Western public.[1] This is not the place to ponder the causes of the GDR's "non-existence" in Western minds; suffice it to say that the blame for this state of affairs lies partly in Bonn, due to its influence on Western attitudes,[2] and partly in East Berlin, due to the difficulties of travel until relatively recently.

Clearly, to be unaware of the GDR is to have a distorted view of Europe and the world. The GDR is second only to the USSR in economic importance among the members of the Warsaw Pact. Even in world terms it is among the top ten industrial nations.[3] It manufactures a wide variety of industrial goods from equipment used in Soviet space-probes to consumer goods which are exported to the West as well as the East. Its armed forces are thought to be the most efficient of those of the Soviet Union's allies.[4] Its 16·9 million citizens together form a modern society in levels of employment in industry, degree of urbanisation, high levels of education, health and welfare services, and so on.

The GDR is fascinating to study especially because of the comparison it offers with the Federal Republic of Germany (West Germany). Until the end of the Second World War in 1945 the peoples of the two German states were united. Since then each state has risen in a seemingly miraculous manner to be important economically, militarily and, more recently, politically. Although both have done well in sport, the GDR, with its much smaller population, has made an especially remarkable contribution to world sport, particularly since the late 1960s.

To explain East Germany's outstanding achievements in sport is not easy. As the writer found out in Berlin just after the 1976 Olympic Games, East German officials themselves find it difficult to explain. Their people have the German sporting traditions in common with the West Germans, and what are basically the same type of economic, social, political and sports' arrangements as their Warsaw Pact allies. Moreover, no one in Berlin doubted that the GDR's recent victories in the world of sport were the result of experience gained before

1945 as well as the great efforts made since that time. And in order to understand sport in the German Democratic Republic today, we must consider the organisation and achievements of pre-1945 Germany in this field.

I. *Historical Development*

(i) *Sport in monarchical Germany*

Arguably the most important influence on the beginnings of modern German sport was Friedrich Ludwig Jahn (1778–1852) who created the first centre for gymnastics in Germany. This was at Berlin in 1811. The idea was to give the young men of Prussia pre-military training at a time when the German states were fighting Napoleonic France. Soon similar centres were set up all over Germany.

After the defeat of Napoleon, reaction triumphed in Prussia and Jahn suffered imprisonment for his allegedly subversive (democratic) ideas. For a time his gymnastics movement was banned. Later, however, the Prussian authorities recognised its potential value to the armed services and it was once again permitted. The movement was split over the abortive democratic revolution of 1848 but, gradually, like German liberalism, it put national unity before democracy and came to terms with the Prussian-dominated German state of Bismarck after 1871.

The official organisational framework of the gymnastic movement was set up at Coburg in 1860. This was *Die Deutsche Turnerschaft* (DT). By 1864 about 13·2 per cent of the urban male population between the ages of fourteen and sixty belonged to it.[5] In social terms it was mainly a movement of the middle and lower middle classes.

With the rise of the German working-class movement, and especially after the founding of the Social Democratic Party at Gotha in 1875, the basis for another mass sports organisation was developed—that of the working class. The movement was born in Berlin in 1890 with the formation of the "Fichte" Gymnastics Association. The next step was the conference at Gera in May 1893 when thirty-nine delegates from fifty-one clubs representing 3,556 members resolved to establish their own organisation—*Der Arbeiter-Turnerbund Deutschlands* (the Workers' Gymnastic Federation of Germany).[6] Membership of the *Bund* reached 70,700 in 1904.[7]

In the second half of the 19th century, other forms of sport began to take root in Germany largely due to British influence. Already in 1836 an "English Rowing Club" had been set up in Hamburg. Others followed. In 1884 the German Cycling Federation was founded and in the same decade similar organisations for swimming, sailing and ice-skating came into existence. In the 1890s athletics, rugby and soccer associations were formed. The clientele of these new bodies was mainly middle class.

Thus by the time the modern Olympic movement was created (1896) Germany was the scene of considerable and varied sporting activity, and in gymnastics the Germans were in the top class.

Misunderstandings and national rivalries prevented official German bodies such as the DT from taking part in the˙ pre-1914 Olympic Games, but in any case the DT itself was generally opposed to "competition" and therefore was against participation in the Olympics. Even so Germans won medals for the horizontal bar and the parallel bars. The medalists then had difficulties with the DT on their return from Athens. Despite the negative attitude of the DT, a German Olympic movement was gradually built up with increasing official approval. In 1912 Germany sent a team 185 strong to the Stockholm Olympics. They returned with five gold, fourteen silver and six bronze medals.[8] This compared with Britain's ten gold, fifteen silver and fifteen bronze,[9] but it was the Americans who virtually swept the board.

The American victory at Stockholm led to considerable discussion in Germany. Perhaps the Germans could learn something from the Americans as they had previously learned from the British. In the words of the *Vossische Zeitung* of Berlin:

America's triumph at Stockholm is not the triumph of spasmodic training or of organisation, as that term is commonly understood, but the national fruit of the long and systematic inculcation of the athletic spirit in American youth. And by the athletic spirit America means not only the rational, uniform development of the body to the highest state of perfection from boyhood up, but the development of all those qualities of mind which are indispensable to pre-eminence in sports . . . Americans race with their heads as well as with their legs, and their Olympic victories are won on the playgrounds of their school days. This is the only reason that we can give for the monotonous reappearance of the Stars and Stripes at the Stadium mast-head of Stockholm.[10]

The discussion of the reasons for American prowess in sport did not begin and end in the columns of newspapers. In 1913 a four-man delegation from German sports organisations toured the USA for an "on the spot" investigation. It was headed by Carl Diem (1882–1962), general secretary of the *Deutsche Sportbehörde für Athletik* (German Sports Authority for Athletics) or DSBfA. With him went Lieutenant, later General, von Reichenau (1884–1942) who was to become notorious for his utterances linking sport to militarism and nationalism.[11] The German delegation concluded that US successes rested on physical training in schools, universities, well-equipped with sporting facilities and well-qualified coaches.[12]

After Stockholm the next Olympic Games were scheduled for Berlin in 1916 and an Imperial committee was appointed to prepare for it, attempts were made to learn the lessons of 1912. Unfortunately for Diem and his collegeagues, the World War deprived the Germans of this opportunity to show their improved skills and organisational ability. During the war the sporting organisations collaborated even more closely with the military in improving the pre-military training of youth.

The rising industrial state of pre-1914 Germany was pre-eminent in scholarship, science and music but was rapidly achieving a leading place for itself among the top sporting nations. In addition to gymnastics, the fencing fraternities of students and the traditional outdoor pastimes of the aristocracy, all the modern sports were developing. An interest was also growing in hiking and camping. The authorities encouraged all this both morally and financially and established playgrounds and parks. They also established a commission for the scientific investigation of sport and bodily exercise. But unlike the loosely-organised amateur sport of Britain, and the highly-competitive sport of the USA, German sport was more closely connected with ideas of patriotism and militarism. It was also divided by politics.

(ii) New ideals: fitness and beauty

It was only with entry into the League of Nations in 1926 and readmission to the Amsterdam Olympics in 1928 that Germany started once again to play a role in international sport. By that time interest in sport had become more widespread than ever before. Writing in 1930 two American educationalists commented:

The first request of the German schoolboy upon meeting a traveller from across the Atlantic is always, "Tell us about sports in America!" Such eagerness to learn about play and physical education in a foreign country reveals one of the outstanding traits of the German people today—their enthusiasm for sports and recreation. Young and old alike seem to have embarked upon a passionate crusade for health and renewed vitality.[13]

It is also worth recording, in view of the Nazi propaganda-picture of German youth and how outsiders "swallowed" it, that in 1930 under the Weimar Republic,

The whole German nation is striving toward a new ideal—physical fitness and beauty. Already one sees marked progress towards this goal. In place of the well-known corpulent type of German boy and girl one now finds slender individuals, lithe, vigorous, enthusiastic—German youth of today.[14]

One ominous note our two American witnesses were forced to strike was political rivalry in sport.

Every social caste and political party, from the conservative to the communist, devotes much time and attention to the athletic and sport phases of its organisation. Both proletarian and monarchist leaders insist that the athletic field is the best recruiting and training ground for their young members . . . Religious groups also make recreation a large part of their programme. Protestant, Catholic, Jewish and non-sectarian organisations vie for control of the children's free time.[15]

In 1928, the workers' sports movement, largely under Social Democratic control, claimed some two million members. It had its own training school at Leipzig which had been partly built with state aid. In 1928 the Communist elements split off to form their own movement. This *Kampfgemeinschaft für rote Sporteinheit* had an estimated 113,542 members in December 1931.[16]

It is virtually impossible to say now to what extent such rivalries in sport adversely affected Germany's performance in international competition. Suffice it to say here that, for whatever reason, Germany's team at Los Angeles in 1932 failed to achieve anything like the level of success achieved at Amsterdam.

In spite of the *débâcle* at Los Angeles much progress had been made in the Weimar Republic in German sport, and this must not be forgotten when evaluating future successes.

(iii) *Hitler's Olympics*

When Hitler gained power in January 1933 many sports officials in Germany felt that they could look forward to much greater state help than before. In his *Mein Kampf* the Nazi leader had recognised the importance of sport and physical training as a matter of national importance. And it had been part and parcel of the Nazi movement, even more than its political rivals, to emphasise physical culture. Indeed, the Nazis consciously placed the physical above the intellectual. There were also many personal connections between the main German sports organisations and the Nazi movement.[17]

Some members of the German sporting community, however, were worried lest the Nazis' well-known aversion to competing against negroes and other *"Untermenschen"* would rob them of their chance to play host to the world's sportsmen. Such elements need not have worried them. Hitler rated propaganda even higher than he rated sport and he was determined to gain the maximum positive publicity from the 1936 Games. He therefore agreed to accept all members of all foreign teams, irrespective of their ethnic origins, on terms of equality. He even attempted to hoodwink the international community by seeming to agree to Jews being members of the German team.

To their credit many, probably the majority of American sports organisations wanted to boycott the Games scheduled in Berlin. But Avery Brundage, Chairman of the American National Olympic Committee, won a 58:56 majority at the conference of the powerful (American) Athletic Union. Without the Americans the Olympic Games would have been a farce.

By the time the 1936 Olympics took place, the German sports movement had been thoroughly Nazified. The working-class organisations were smashed in 1933, and the bourgeois organisations, DRA and DT, attempted to reorganise themselves in line with Nazi principles. This, however, did not save them from extinction. The Nazis restructured German sport into a centralised body of fifteen sections representing the various branches of sport. Most of the old functionaries, including Diem, were given employment in the new organisation. The other outstanding organiser of German sport in the Weimar Republic, Theodor Lewald, had to go since he was a Jew, although the Nazis used him in their international sporting relations for a time because of his symbolic value as much as his unrivalled knowledge and connections. In 1934 German sport was again re-organised in the *Deutscher Reichsbund für Leibesübungen* (DRL) comprising twenty-one centrally-run divisions.

From the Nazi point of view the 1936 Olympics were value for money. They must go down as one of the biggest propaganda victories in history. The Nazis worked hard to make them a success. Money was no object. The organisational experience gained at successive Nuremburg rallies was effectively put into use. Leni Reifenstahl, who had so cleverly filmed those rallies, was once again called in to record the Games. Hitler ordered all Government bodies to give sportsmen in their employ unlimited time-off to train, and the DRL put on intensive training sessions. The Nazis were rewarded for their efforts with, in terms of medals, outright victory: Germany rose from sixth place in 1932 to first place in 1936. Even so they did not succeed in making much impression in athletics, a traditionally weak area for Germany. And it was American athletes, especially Jesse Owens, winner of the 100m., 200m., and long jump, who captured the imagination of the sporting public.

In the years after 1936 the DRL and the Hitler Youth put increasing emphasis on para-military sports—gliding, parachute-jumping, rifle-shooting, motor-cycling, grenade-throwing. But the more traditional forms of sporting activity were still carried on. German teams still competed abroad. In 1938, for instance, official German teams took part in fixtures in twenty-six countries, seventeen in France and fourteen in Poland among them. Tennis and golf continued to be played and Gottfried von Cramm continued his tennis exploits to the approval of the international tennis community. Max Schmelling won renown in boxing. German motor-racing drivers also made a good reputation for themselves in the years before the war.

Germany was a relatively late developer in sport compared with Britain. But it had certain traditional strengths, above all in gymnastics. State encouragement, for military, economic, political and ideological reasons, became a key factor in the development of German sport under successive regimes. The attempt to improve sporting performance by the application of science and medicine was in line with the importance given to science in German society generally. Both these features distinguished German sport from that in Britain. Mass participation in sports clubs which, in part at least, reflected patriotic, political and religious concerns, as well as the normal interest in recreational activities, was another distinguishing feature. Sectarian rivalries tended to stimulate participation before 1933. There is little doubt that social pressure did so after that date.

Postwar Germany therefore inherited many experienced sports administrators (even if depleted by war losses), the recognition of medicine and science as aids to sport, pride in the recent achievements of German sport, and widespread acceptance of sport, and of participation in sport, as something positive in modern society. All this must be kept continually in mind when examining the sporting attainments of the German Democratic Republic.

(iv) *Sport under occupation*

As sport had been closely associated with military preparedness, indoctrination and the glorification of the Nazi state, it was only to be expected that the four Allied powers would outlaw existing sports organisations and severely restrict sporting activities. Under Directive No. 23 of the Allied Control Commission, the pre-occupation sports organisations were banned, as was the practising of para-military sport. The directive restricted sporting activity to organisations based purely on the locality (*Kreis*), and then only with the permission of the local allied military commandant.

Remarkably, sporting activity suffered only a very brief interruption. In Dortmund, in the British Zone, in July 1945, the Borussia Association met and elected as its leading officers non-Nazis. These officials were then confirmed by the British and Borussia commenced with a limited football programme.[18] In the Soviet Zone a start was made in the same month to renovating the stadium in Spindlerfeld, East Berlin by

Soviet soldiers, old workers' sports activists and friends from the former bourgeois sport movement.[19]

Quite soon in both parts of Germany some regular sports activity was under way. In the West the situation differed from zone to zone, but in general the three Allies sought to influence German sports development in a decentralised, non-political, non-sectarian, direction. This was partly achieved through the system of licensing—all German organisations required the approval of the appropriate occupying power before they could legally operate. The result was that sporting bodies tended to be specialist clubs for particular sports, as they had been before 1945, but first on a local, and then on a regional (*Land*) basis. Their officials were often those who had served in the same capacity under the Nazis, as they had the expertise. The working-class sports movement, despite much discussion, was not re-established.

In the Soviet Zone sports activity on an organised basis was virtually confined to the Free German Youth and the trade unions. The Free German Youth (FDJ) was set up in 1946 and, like the trade unions, was under Communist direction. From the start it was part of the FDJ's strategy to win German youth for its political ideals by lavish provision for sport, by providing them with facilities in short supply or too expensive for individuals to provide for themselves. The writer well remembers seeing FDJ literature in the late 1940s and early 1950s which underlined this point, and was impressed by the apparent lavishness of sports facilities in East Germany in 1951.

Of necessity, many of the old officials of the Nazi sports organisation were able to use their expertise in the new movement, though often supervised by Communists.

(v) *Following the Soviet model*

As it became clear that a new state was to be erected in the Soviet Zone, moves were made to establish a sports organisation which would fulfil the aspirations of that state in sport. In August 1948 the *Deutscher Sportausschuss* (German Sports Committee) or DSA was announced. A resolution adopted by the ruling Socialist Unity Party (SED) on 17 March 1951 set out the position of the DSA as the supreme organ in all fields of sport and physical culture in the German Democratic Republic.[20] According to this document the DSA had a virtual monopoly-position in regard to sport in the new Republic. It was put in charge of all educational institutions concerned with sport, of all sports activities in schools and universities, and was responsible for all research work in this field. Further, it played an important role in the treatment of sport in the mass media. It initiated and checked the production of all sports equipment and, together with the appropriate ministries, was responsible for the building of stadia, playing fields, etc. The actual organisations engaged in sports activities were to remain the trade unions and the FDJ. Each trade union belonging to the Free German Trade Union Federation (FDGB) was responsible for building up its own sports association (*Sportvereinigung*) or SV. There were some fifteen of these.[21] Thus there was, for example, *SV Aktivist* covering the mining industry, *SV Lokomotive* for railway employees, and *SV Fortschritt* (Progress) for those employed in the textile and leather industries. In addition, *SV Dynamo* enrolled members of the police.[22]

Even at this time attempts were made to make sport in the GDR something of a mass activity. The March 1951 Resolution[23] claimed that some 750,000 members were in the "Democratic Sports Movement". This was in a country which at that time had a population of some 18·3 millions.

Apart from the generous provision of equipment, how were the GDR leaders achieving this mass participation? A number of measures had been introduced under the *Gesetz über die Teilnahme der Jugend am Aufbau der Deutschen Demokratischen Republik* (Law Concerning the Participation of Youth in the Building of the German Democratic Republic) of 8 February 1950.[24] Section VII of the Law laid down that all state organs were required to help in the development of the Democratic Sports Movement, physical education and hiking. In more concrete terms, it established a Sports Insignia (countrywide uniform sports programme) of the GDR, pledged increases in the production of sports equipment, clothing and footwear. A number of key sports complexes were to be built, restored or expanded. Among these were the now famous *Hochschule für Körperkultur* (University for Physical Culture) in Leipzig (see below), the sports school at Hamberge, Bad Blankenburg and Werdau, the Hallen Swimming Baths at Rostock, the stadia at Schwerin, Anker-Wismar, Frankfurt (Oder), Cottbus, Finsterwalde, and, among other projects, the ice-rink at Berlin, and the gliding establishment at Magdeburg. In addition to the development of the *Hochschule* at Leipzig with an initial intake of 400 students, other university-level institutions were to be developed. Finally, rail fare reductions of 50 per cent on journeys of up to 100 km, and 75 per cent on journeys over 100 km, were offered to sports participants.

The SED Resolution of 1951, referred to above, made further concrete proposals to improve the sports capacity of the GDR. It announced the setting-up of special boarding schools for children of fourteen and over who had a special talent for sport. Whilst these schools would provide a general education, they would place much more emphasis on sport. The Resolution also called for compulsory sport in all trade-union and factory-based schools. Two other key sections of the Resolution were devoted to the *Hochschule* at Leipzig and to the Sports Insignia. It added "German" to its official name, called for a speed-up of its development, recognised it as a university with the right to confer degrees (*Staatsexamen*), and gave it a central role in research in this field.

The Resolution laid down that there were to be three stages in the awards for the Sports Insignia.:

1. 10–14 year-olds: "Be Ready for Peace and Friendship among the Peoples" badge.
2. 14–16 year-olds: "Be Ready to Work and Defend Peace" badge
3. 16–18 year-olds: "Ready to Work and Defend Peace" badge.*

The Resolution did not lay down the actual standards to be achieved or the conditions for qualification. It did permit those over eighteen to qualify at all three levels and it called for the sports movement to aim for top international standards.

Already by 1950–1, sport in the GDR was exhibiting certain characteristics which had been noticed in German sport in the 1933–45 period. It was centrally organised. It was based on a monopolistic youth movement and monopolistic labour organisations owing allegiance to a monopolistic political party, the SED.[25] It was carrying on the tradition of scientific study of sport. And it was identified with the state.

The SED document of 17 March 1951 strongly emphasised the political involvement of sport in the GDR. It started with the following declaration:

The German Democratic Republic forms the basis for the solution of the tasks placed before the German people in the struggle to secure peace, and to secure the unity of a peace-loving, democratic and independent Germany. Its consolidation and strengthening is, therefore, a significant contribution to the struggle against the US imperialists and their German agents, who, especially through re-militarisation and through preparations for a new war, severely endanger the German nation.

The activities of the Democratic Sports Movement are bound up with the great tasks which the Government and all the progressive forces of our German Democratic Republic have set themselves . . . The task of the German Democratic Sports Movement is therefore to educate people who are ready to work and to defend peace.[26]

The word "defend" was not loosely used, and was to become of great significance in the following years and beyond.

After dealing with the organisation of sport in the GDR, as outlined above, the Resolution ended strongly with the following political message:

---

* These badges were very similar to the "Be Ready for Labour and Defence" (10–16 year olds) and "Ready for Labour and Defence" (16–18 year olds) then existing in the USSR. [Ed.]

We must aim, in more significant measure than before, to learn from the sportsmen of the Soviet Union and the People's Democracies and, above all, to evaluate the scientific experience of Soviet sport for the development of the Democratic Sports Movement.

It is the task of the DSA to establish even closer ties with the sports committees of the Peoples Democracies, in order to organise joint training courses with the sportsmen of these countries.

With the fulfilment of these tasks, the sportsmen and women of the people's sports movement of our German Democratic Republic join in the great world-encompassing front of peace.

In this way they express their readiness, in keeping with their slogan "Ready to Work and to Defend Peace", to take the cause of peace firmly in their hands and, side by side with the Soviet Union, headed by the standard-bearer of peace, Generalissimo Stalin, actively to defend it to the utmost.

At this time, 1950–2, the Soviet/SED political line in Germany was to use the GDR as the nucleus for a re-united Germany, re-united therefore on Soviet terms. To this end a strong SED force was to be built up in all spheres. These people, speaking as one voice, would then have a strong, even dominant position, in any inter-German assemblies, commissions or committees. As the March 1951 SED Resolution indicated, sport was regarded as a key area through which the youth of the West, as well as the East, could be attracted to the Communist ideal. The DSA was given the task of "winning tens of thousands of young sportsmen from West Germany for participation in the Third World Festival Games of Youth and Students for Peace". The Resolution, in complete contrast to the SED's later view, also called for the establishment of an all-German National Olympic Committee (NOK). This was not achieved, and in 1955 the GDR set up its own NOK. The World Festival Games were held in Berlin in the summer of 1951 as part of the World Youth Festival. They were surrounded by cold war confrontation. Western governments attempted to prevent their youth from taking part, and from West Berlin the participants were subjected to a barrage of propaganda, including an armada of propaganda balloons. The Games did attract some young people from West Germany and Western Europe, and in fact provided an opportunity for the Soviet Union to demonstrate its sporting skill. From the GDR's point of view, they showed that the youth organisation, the FDJ, which was responsible for running the Games, had inherited, and was maintaining, the German tradition for superb organisation.[27]

In July 1952, another step was taken to centralise the administration of sport. This was with the establishment of *Das Staatliche Komitee für Körperkultur und Sport* (The State Committee for Physical Culture and Sport). It was officially designated the highest sports authority in the GDR and its chairman and his deputy were both appointed by the

Government, the GDR Council of Ministers. The DSA continued in existence. The setting-up of this committee indicated once again the importance attached to sport by the SED. It also indicated some dissatisfaction with the results so far and the new tasks to come. One of these new tasks was the development of para-military sport in the GDR.

(vi) *Military training through sport*

The work of fostering interest in para-military sport was given to a new body *Die Gesellschaft für Sport und Technik*—GST (The Society for Sport and Technology). Set up in August 1952, it was modelled directly on the Soviet civil defence organisation—*DOSAAF*. Under the control of the Ministry of the Interior the GST was required to develop interest in gliding, flying, model flying, parachute-jumping, motoring and motor cycling, sea sports involving navigation, signals and diving, shooting, tracking and map-reading, the use of radio transmitters and animal-training sports (horses, dogs and carrier pigeons).

The setting up of the GST was an integral part of the military build-up of the armed forces of the GDR which was announced in 1952. The GST initially attracted considerable interest among young people. Once again there was the chance to engage in hobbies which were exciting and beyond the means of most young people. By the end of 1952, the Society had, according to one Western estimate, 500,000 members.[28] But because of the political upheavals of 1953–4 and the increasing emphasis on the more military side of its activities, membership slumped. By the mid-1960s, however, membership was once again around the half million mark; because of the social pressures to join, and the advantages membership can offer to those who, since 1962, have to do military service anyway, it is likely to be even higher today.

Although aimed mainly at young people, originally anyone could join the GST, but since 1955 it has been restricted to young men and women between the ages of fourteen and twenty-four. This is because since that date there have been other opportunities for part-time military training for those over twenty-four, above all in the factory *Kampfgruppen* (fighting groups) first organised in 1953–4. Over the years the character of the GST has become more and more military-orientated with the dropping of such non-military sports as those connected with animals. When the Ministry of Defence was organised in 1956, the GST came under its jurisdiction. Active membership of the Society is a virtual necessity for all those hoping to study. The GST holds its own Olympics, involving largely "sports" of direct military utility, with teams competing from the other Warsaw Pact states.[29]

(vii) *The Search for recognition*

In 1957 a number of important changes occurred in sports organisation with the formation of a new body *Der Deutsche Turn- und Sports-bund* (the German Gymnastics and Sports Association), the DTSB, which replaced replaced the DSA. It was thought that the sports movement had become mature enough in both sporting and political terms to benefit from its own separate organisation. The DSA was criticised for not creating a mass sports movement; it appeared incapable of reaching out to those who were put off by the official character of the FDJ or did not want to associate their leisure-time activities with their place of work.

The DTSB was organised on a nationwide basis corresponding to the administrative structure of the GDR. Its structure was supposed to give it flexibility so that it could exploit the existing sports activities of the FDJ and the trade union affiliates, but at the same time involve others not catered for by these activities. The new organisation, with com-mittees at all levels of the GDR's political-administrative structure, incorporated the sports associations of the trade unions at its regional level. In addition, specialist associations were established for the various categories of sport—*Deutscher Turnverband* (German Gymnasts Associa-tion), *Deutscher Verband für Leichtathletik* (German Association for Athletics), *Deutscher Schwimmsportverband* (German Swimming As-sociation), etc.[30]

The work of co-ordinating the various sports activities and assessing priorities was the job of the State Committee on which the DTSB, GST, FDJ, FDGB (trade unions), Ministry of Education, Ministry of Health, Ministries of Defence and the Interior, the Leipzig *Hochschule*, and some other interests were represented.

If there were good sports-technical reasons for this re-organisation in 1957, there were more important political reasons, Though it still called for German re-unification, the SED now sought full recognition of the German Democratic Republic as an equal of the Federal Republic of Germany. If re-unification was ever to be achieved, it could only come through a confederation of the two equal states. In a situation in which the GDR was isolated from the West, its sporting organisations took on special significance. As one West German writer has com-mented:

In the struggle for the international recognition of the GDR, the DTSB with its associations played a very important role long before the GDR was able to break out of its political isolation; GDR sport breached the blockade that at the time of the cold war kept the GDR from almost all international relations outside the Communist states. Because the GDR in its sports achievements reached international standards, and in most areas actually set standards, the international sports organisations were unable to ignore the GDR.[31]

By 1965 all the specialist associations had been granted international recognition. However, their acceptance by international federations was not without much controversy over the exact designation of the country (GDR or East Germany).

GDR's search for recognition in the Olympic movement was subject to similar restrictions. For many years the International Olympic Committee (IOC) was only prepared to allow participation of an all-German team drawn from both German states. This solution the GDR refused to accept in 1952 but it did so in time for the Melbourne Olympics in 1956. At that time there was no problem of national flags as both Germanies had adopted the black-red-gold flag of the Weimar Republic. The IOC cleared the hurdle of national anthems with tact by using the last movement of Beethoven's 9th Symphony. In 1960, the IOC had to decide what to do about the German flag as the GDR had modified its flag by adding a coat of arms. The IOC this time solved the problem by designing a special flag for the all-German team, the traditional black, red and gold flag with the Olympic rings added to it. In 1968, at the Mexico Olympics, the two Germanies were permitted to enter separate teams, whilst the earlier ruling on flags and anthems was retained. It was at the Munich Olympics four years later that the GDR finally achieved its ambition of full international recognition. It is convenient to list here the results of those early Olympic encounters between the two Germans states:[32]

Table 1.   OLYMPIC RESULTS, FRG AND GDR
1952–60 OLYMPIC GAMES

	Gold		Silver		Bronze	
	FRG	GDR	FRG	GDR	FRG	GDR
Oslo (Winter 1952)	3	—	2	—	2	—
Helsinki (Summer 1952)	—	—	7	—	17	—
Cortina d'Ampezzo (Winter 1956)	1	—	—	—	—	1
Melbourne (Summer 1956)	5	1	9	4	6	2
Squaw Valley (Winter 1960)	2	2	2	1	1	—
Rome (Summer 1960)	10	3	10	9	6	7

These results revealed the absolute superiority of the West Germans during the 1950s. The gap was though closed towards the end of the period, and, on a relative-to-population basis, certainly by the Rome Olympics, the GDR had overtaken its Western rival. How did the SED evaluate the results?

The Fifth Congress of the SED in July 1958 led to criticisms of the work of the sports movement. The Congress had adopted the proposal of its First Secretary, Walter Ulbricht (1893–1973), that the GDR should overtake West Germany in *per capita* production of important industrial goods by 1960. The SED was merely following the Soviet party, which had promised its people that it would overtake the USA by 1960 To say the least, both promises proved to be wildly unrealistic. Nevertheless, the DSA Chairman, Rudi Reichert[33] felt compelled to make a similar promise in regard to East German sport in its competition with the West Germans. Having been criticised by Ulbricht he also admitted defects in the work of the DTSB. For years, he revealed, the membership of the DTSB had remained at about 1·3 million. He said that too much emphasis was put on providing facilities for existing members and not enough on winning new ones. Even among existing members funds were often spent on particular (minority) activities, to the detriment of the mass of the members. Sports officials were accused of working bureaucratically in that they remained officebound, and did not get out to try to interest those outside the official sports movement. Finally, Herr Reichert accused some of this colleagues of looking too much to the West for their standards instead of remembering the SED slogan "To learn from the Soviet Union is to learn to be victorious".[34]

The delegates had heard the substance of the criticisms and of the promises before. Probably they remained somewhat sceptical. In sport, however, the GDR was more or less on target in 1960. Nevertheless Herr Ulbricht and his colleagues in the Politburo seem to have concluded that changes were needed at the top of the GDR sports movement. In May 1961, Manfred Ewald[35] took over from Rudi Reichert as President of the DTSB. It is under his administration that the DTSB and its affiliates have achieved their spectacular successes but clearly much had already been achieved under Herr Reichert's leadership.

Let us pause, again, to take stock of the GDR's Olympic advances in the 1960s:[36]

Table 2. OLYMPIC RESULTS, FRG AND GDR, 1964–68

| | Gold | | Silver | | Bronze | |
	FRG	GDR	FRG	GDR	FRG	GDR
Tokyo (1964)	7	3	15	7	12	6
Mexico (1968)	5	9	11	9	10	7

II. Sport and physical education in schools

In spite of all the extra-curricular opportunities for physical recreation in the GDR, the school remains the institution through which most children receive their introduction to sport. This aspect of education, no less than all others, has been the subject of continuous scrutiny and re-assessment.

Just as much as other aspects of education, physical education in the Soviet Zone of Germany suffered greatly at the end of the war. Buildings were damaged or destroyed, equipment was not available, there was a shortage of suitable teachers, and the children were often in no condition to exert themselves physically. Of the 11,000 prewar schools in the Soviet Zone outside Berlin, 134 were totally destroyed, 363 badly damaged, and 2,741 lightly damaged. In Berlin the situation was much worse. In addition, many of the school buildings were taken over by the occupation/administrative authorities for other purposes.[37]

In theory every school class was to have two hours per week of physical exercise, one afternoon per week was to be set aside for games, and once a month a country hike was to be organised. There were no innovations in the field of physical training.[38] Despite many gallant efforts on the part of conscientious teachers, this regulation could not be rigorously implemented. Standards varied greatly according to local circumstances, and not much attention appears to have been paid to physical education before 1950.[39]

During the early 1950s, far more attention was attached to physical education and games in schools. Physical education became a "major" subject, meaning that certain minimum standards of achievement were required of all pupils. The reason for this renewed interest was probably twofold. Firstly, as the basic problems of the early years had been solved, more attention could be given to so-called secondary subjects. The other reason for the renewed interest in sport was political: the SED's interest in promoting military preparedness. As in the general sports movement, so too in GDR schools, the Free German Youth and the trade unions were given much of the responsibility for realising the SED's aims. With varying degrees of emphasis, depending on the changing political situation, the SED stressed sports of military utility to the neglect of others. The regime faced the opposition of teachers, pupils and parents. Certainly this was one of the reasons which caused large numbers of teachers to migrate to the West. Between 1952 and 1959, some 13,852 school teachers left the Republic.[40] The seriousness of this may be seen in the light of the figure of only 6,095 students studying to be teachers in 1957.[41]

The 20th Congress of the Communist Party of the Soviet Union in 1956 brought a certain relaxation in the Soviet Union, which was followed by similar changes in the German Democratic Republic. Whether a direct result of this trend, or independent of it, the setting-up of the DTSB in 1957 brought changes in school sport. The role of the GST was reduced in favour of the DTSB and military sports suffered a setback in the schools.[42]

The late 1950s and early 1960s brought a more realistic appraisal of the opportunities and limitations of school sport. The fact was that many schools still did not have the facilities to engage in sophisticated sports training and physical education. And though there had been a great improvement since the founding of the Republic, there was still a shortage of appropriately-trained, specialist teachers. The regulations covering secondary school examinations in physical education published in January 1963 made some concessions to local conditions and local initiative. These examinations were, and are, compulsory for all children[43] on leaving school at either sixteen, the minimum age for leaving, or at eighteen, for the 13 per cent who stay on to that age.[44] Under these regulations the head-teachers were given the main responsibility for the examinations. The examination boards comprised the school head, or deputy head, the form teacher, the physical education teacher and appropriate arbiters. It was recommended that, in the interests of objective assessment, several schools in a neighbourhood should get together to conduct the exams. These physical education exams were divided into three parts. The first mark was to be given for a series of exercises designed to test the pupil's strength, speed, agility, stamina and suppleness. The second part was divided between winter sports and team games—soccer, handball, basketball or volleyball. The particular game was left to the school to choose. Part three was made up of athletics and swimming. The regulations recognised that in some schools it would be impossible to award any mark for swimming because no swimming facilities existed. These regulations admit the possibility of considerable differences of standards in different schools and in different parts of the country. But the children would all get the same certificates.[45]

One feature of these regulations was the potential influence they gave to the civil defence organisation, the GST. Should a pupil not come up to standard on the day, the examination board was empowered to consider his or her extra-curricular sports activities in the GST. And one cannot help feeling that such activities would weigh heavily in the pupil's favour.

It is also clear from many other regulations, speeches and announcements, that the GST remained an organisation of great importance throughout the 1960s and up to the present time. If anyone was in doubt, a joint announcement of the Ministry of Education and the Central Council of the GST on 18 March 1963 removed any such doubt:

The socialist defence training (*Wehrerziehung*) of our youth is an integral part of socialist education. It is of great importance for the youth of the German Democratic Republic, serving to strengthen our Workers' and Peasants' State and therefore to secure peace.

It once again stressed that this work demanded the close co-operation of the Ministry of Education, the FDJ and the GST. It listed a number of measures needed to improve this pre-military training. The most important of these was the setting-up of branches of the GST at all schools with the aim of drawing all children of 15 and over into such training. It also called for the inclusion of military sports in schools' sports days.[46]

The renewed[47] emphasis on pre-military training of East German youth was permissible owing to the changed situation since the 1950s. In the earlier period there was a good deal of opposition to military sports. A number of young people had voted with their feet by going West. In August 1961, the building of the Berlin Wall had put a stop to that. Shortly after its erection the SED felt it could at last introduce conscription. The leadership of the ruling Socialist Unity Party no doubt believed the time was ripe to step up the campaign for the military training of youth in schools as well.

With so much official emphasis on sports of military utility, with pressure on pupils to join the GST[48], one wonders just how successful the Society has been in achieving its objects, and whether GST work has assisted in the GDR's rise to world status as an Olympic power. It is easier to pose the question than to answer it. According to official figures, in the 14 to 16 age-group, 37,572 children were awarded the badge "Ready to Work and to Defend the Homeland" in 1957. The number rose to 55,608 in 1962—i.e. approximately 11 per cent of all 14–16 year-olds, since the number of children in the relevant age groups was about 500,000.[49] The numbers taking these awards have risen steadily. In the year 1975–6, the figure was 79,612.[50] In spite of these apparent successes, the authorities have not always been satisfied with the level of physical training of national-service recruits.[51] It has to be remembered that since girls do not undergo national service, sport within the GST is a means of military preparation for them.

Taking physical education in East German schools as a whole, one cannot but admire the way in which the tremendous difficulties of the immediate postwar years were overcome, and the great strides which have been made since then. However, it would be naive to suppose that all the Republic's schools have the facilities of some schools which have been visited by foreign educationalists. Gaps still remain. There are still a considerable number of schools with inadequate physical training facilities. GDR figures indicate that in 1968 there were only 3,358 gymnasia for the Republic's 7,749 schools of all types.[52] There

PLATES

Acknowledgments: 1–4, Society for Cultural Relations with the U.S.S.R., London; 5–7, Prof. H. Bäskau, Wilhelm-Pieck University, Rostock, G.D.R.; 8, 9, Dr Vladimir Kostka; 11–15, Anglo-Chinese Educational Institute, London; 16, 17, Roy A. Clumpner; 18–22, Ron Pickering.

THE U.S.S.R.

4

THE G.D.R.

5

6

7

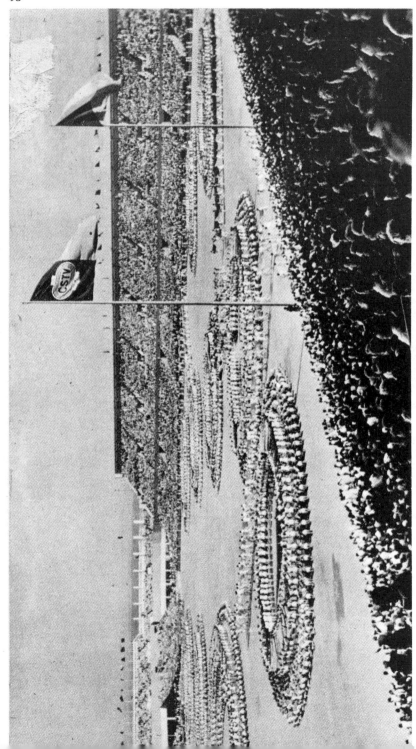

16

17

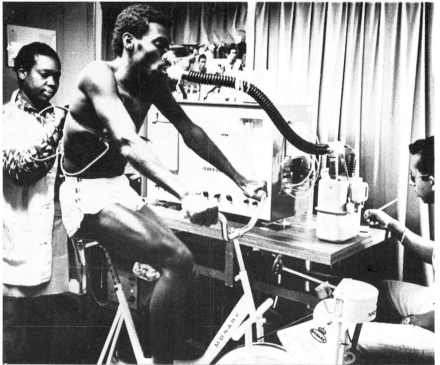

22

were great variations according to region. Berlin's 208 schools had 194 gymnasia. In Schwerin, on the other hand, there were only ninety-four for 413 schools, while Neubrandenburg's 610 schools were equipped with a mere seventy-eight. No doubt to some extent this problem is being overcome by using facilities belonging to the DTSB, FDJ and other bodies. Provision of all-year swimming facilities is another area of some difficulty, although here it is claimed that camps run during the holidays, which provide intensive and free swimming instruction, have virtually overcome this problem. But in 1968 it was admitted that nearly 10 per cent of NVA recruits could not swim.[53] The GDR's difficulty in swimming facilities becomes clear when a comparison with West Germany is made. In 1969 the GDR possessed eighty-eight indoor swimming baths, West Germany 628. In the same year the GDR had 1,687 outdoor and indoor swimming pools, while West Germany had 5,108. Even allowing for the difference in population the GDR was well behind the Federal Republic in its provision for swimming facilities.[54]

Despite all the progress made, it is unlikely that the GDR's normal school system, even with the help of the GST, has been the basis for its recent Olympic successes—although it is certainly no handicap compared with the situation in many other states.

One method used to involve young people in sport and improve their sports performance has been the sports competitions (Spartakiaden) carried out every year throughout the GDR. Started in 1965, these competitions are the joint responsibility of the Ministry of Education, the DTSB, the FDJ and its junior component, the Young Pioneers. They are carried through at all levels of the Republic with the winners going through to the next stage. In 1969, 65,600 young competitors reached the fifteen regional Spartakiade. In 1973, the number was 92,500.[55] These competitions are treated very seriously by the GDR's sporting and youth organisations, and are given a great deal of publicity in the mass media. Most of the GDR's athletes who have succeeded in recent international sports events have previously been winners at national level in the Spartakiaden. Moreover, the Spartakiade are used to spot sporting talent and invite promising young athletes to join a sports school.

The special sports schools, mentioned above, are another means of boosting the sporting achievements of the Republic's young people. Established in 1952 (just three years after the GDR's foundation) these schools remain few in number. By 1958-9 there were twenty-two of them,[56] which is roughly the number today. Outstanding among these schools is the "Artur Becker" School at Dresden. Its most famous former pupil is Ulrike Richter, who won three golds at the 1976 Olympics with three record-breaking swims. Another famous former pupil is Christa Scheiblich, 1976 Olympic gold medalist in the women's single sculls. According to official publications, the idea is to spot children who, being members of the FDJ or Young Pioneers, are specially gifted in a particular sport and then give them the chance to transfer to a school which can help them to develop their special talents. As one publication put it:

They are of a comprehensive character and have exactly the same responsibilities for the upbringing of the younger generation as all other schools; but in addition they train their pupils to become first class sportsmen and sportswomen of great versatility. Many of the pupils from these schools choose by preference sporting professions or those related to them, although the latter choice of profession is not a condition for admission to such schools.[57]

The Education Law of 1965 did, however, rather more than this earlier statement, seem to link them with a more vocational orientation:

Special schools are general schools. They serve the special requirements of providing skilled people for the economy, science, sport and culture. The special schools admit pupils with high performances and special talents.[58]

Like the other special residential schools for Russian, music and mathematics, the sports schools (KJS) have been criticised from time to time as élite institutions running counter to the GDR's idea of comprehensive education. One sometimes hears, too, that some children gain entry to these schools by virtue of their connections rather than because of their special abilities.

In the sports schools the pupils are given intensive coaching in their chosen sport; the sports practised in the schools are, in fact, confined to a narrow range of Olympic sports only. As much of their time is taken up with sport, pupils who wish to obtain the *Abitur*, the school-leaving certificate necessary for university matriculation, often have to remain at school for a year or two extra.

These KJS have had many successes, and are clearly a key part of the system for producing winning athletes. The other parts of that system are the specialist institutions and organisations in the Republic—the sports clubs of the armed forces and the police, the *Deutsche Hochschule für Körperkultur*, and the other university-level institutions providing sports education.

III. *Army and police sports clubs*

The sports organisations of the East German armed forces and of the People's Police hold a place of paramount importance in the GDR sports system. Because of their sensitive defence connections, not much has been published about them, apart that is, from purely propaganda/publicity material. The Central Army Sports Club (ZASK), otherwise known as *Vorwärts*, has played a major part in the GDR's international sports offensive since it was set up in 1956. In 1974, it had some 180,000 members, which was more than the official strength of the armed forces at that time. Between 1956 and 1974 its members won 122 gold, 110 silver and 114 bonze medals at the Olympic Games, world and European championships. At the Munich Olympics in 1972, it accounted for 54 members of the GDR's 330-strong team. Its present chairman is Admiral Waldemar Berner.

The sports club of the People's Police and Security Police (SSD)— *Dynamo*—was established in 1953. Headed by Erich Mielke, member of the Politburo and Minister of State Security, it had 230,000 members in 1974. About 90,000 members were children or young people. Up to 1974, *Dynamo* had forty-two gold, seventy-two silver and sixty-six bronze medals to its credit in Olympic and other international encounters.[59] *Dynamo* has been particularly successful with its women competitors, the most famous of whom in recent years is Karin Janz, the gymnast who won a silver and a bronze in Mexico in 1968, and two golds, two silvers and a bronze at Munich. Monika Zehrt is another product of this club. She won a gold in the 400m. athletics event at Munich in 1972 and was one of the GDR's world record-breakers in the 4 × 400m.

These two clubs are key components in the GDR's system for training top-flight athletes. With their close links with the Politburo they would seem to be in a strong position when consideration of their financial needs comes up for discussion.

IV. *Deutsche Hochschule für Körperkulter*

Reference has already been made to the *Deutsche Hochschule für Körperkultur* (German University for Physical Culture), the DHfK. Set up in 1950 with ninety-six students, fourteen full-time and a number of part-time members of staff, the DHfK had over 2,000 students and 300 staff members in 1975.[60] Its main aim is to educate and train teachers of physical education, coaches and sports officials, and to engage in research into all aspects of sport and physical education. It also has certain responsibilities for helping to develop the sports life of Leipzig. One of its functions, of considerable political as well as educational importance, is to assist in training sports personnel from abroad. These are mainly from third world states, including Cuba. They usually undergo an eight-month course at the DHfK, after which a few then take the regular course. This regular course for GDR students lasts four years, at the end of which students receive a diploma, the equivalent of a B.A. or B.Sc. degree. The biggest single component of the course is physical education in all its ramifications. After this,

Marxism–Leninism is the single most important subject; it is studied throughout the four years and takes up 300 hours of the students' timetable. Other subjects include two foreign languages (one of which has to be Russian), mathematics and cybernetics, science, logic, sports medicine, and the theory and history of sport. The best students may obtain a doctorate after three years' postgraduate research.

A British educationalist, David Johnston, wrote after a visit to the DHfK,

This is one of the most remarkable institutions in the whole of the GDR. It is certainly unique in its treatment of physical culture. There is probably no college, or, more literally, no university in the whole world that may stand comparison with it.

This English visitor felt that the participation by DHfK students in the classes of the neighbouring Karl Marx University was just one sign of its full university status. He was also very impressed by its buildings and equipment.

The generosity of the policy of equipping the DHfK and the scientific, analytical and objective mode of study and research are both illustrated by the way in which the use of the cine-camera is planned as a normal aid to the study and presentation of the dynamics of movement. The commitment to the view that physical fitness contributes to public health may be seen from the way future organisers of physical education in factories, the youth service or in regions are trained alongside future teachers.[61]

Though unique in its own way, the DHfK is by no means the only university-level institution in the GDR giving higher education in sport. Sport-Wissenschaft (sports science) is taught as a separate discipline, at the universities of Berlin, Greifswald, Halle, Jena, Rostock, as well as the university-level teacher training establishments at Potsdam Halle-Kröllwitz and Zwickau.

Apart from those studying physical education and sport as a regular university subject, all physically-healthy students are obliged to take part in sporting activities for the first three years of their course. When this was first introduced as a compulsory subject in 1951/2 only 41 per cent of the students at the Berlin Humboldt University took part. At Leipzig, 60 per cent did so, but at Greifswald the percentage was as low as 40. By 1955/6 the great majority of students were taking part. Today virtually all do so.[62] Although it is difficult to be precise about the standards achieved, as in all GDR sports work, training programmes are, in fact, based on international standards.

Official sources claim that in 1975, 64·6 per cent of full-time students took part in military sports competitions.[63] But according to official documents this is just one reason for making sport compulsory at universities. The general improvement of the physical capabilities of the students is the reason most often given. Second in importance is said to be character-training in such traits as team-spirit, decisiveness, perseverance, discipline, daring, honesty, and the ability to be self-critical and to judge oneself.[64]

V. *Sports medicine*

Another example of how serious the GDR authorities take sport is indicated by the introduction of specialist doctors for sport (*Sportarzt*) in 1963. Like other aspects of sports development in the German Democratic Republic this follows the Soviet pattern. The training for this profession is four years upon completion of general medical training. There are probably somewhere in the region of 600–700 sports doctors in the GDR. They have their own organisation, the *Gesellschaft für Sportmedizin der DDR*, which co-operates closely with the DHfK and other appropriate bodies. Most of these doctors are employed by the health authorities of the GDR's fifteen administrative districts (*Bezirke*) and have the job of supervising the medical aspects of sport in the schools and in the various sports organisations. A few are employed by clubs and organisations direct. As with some other facilities, these doctors are concentrated in the major urban centres and better-endowed clubs. It is a measure of official esteem in which sports medicine is held that several doctors and other medical staff involved in sport have been decorated with the Hufeland Medal for their services to sport.[65]

As a rule, the medics work closely with P.E. instructors and sports coaches, although often the latter themselves are well-versed in sports medicine. Unlike many of their colleagues in the West, the GDR's coaches are the product of a thorough education in sports-related subjects. As one British sportswriter put it in relation to the GDR's swimming successes:

Although there is always a doctor on the pool-side to assist the coach, what makes the relationship between the two supervisors sometimes so different from Western countries is that the coach is sufficiently versed in the principles of physiology to understand the reasons behind the doctors' recommendations.[66]

It was perhaps the work of the East German doctors and coaches which caused some doubts about the GDR's methods among some Western competitors and officials in Montreal in 1976. Criticism of the physical appearance of some GDR lady swimmers must be treated with some circumspection. To be sure, some criticisms are the product of jealousy, professional rivalry and wounded pride. Nonetheless, some eminent people have cast doubt upon the issue: the distinguished West German sports doctor, Professor Adolf Metzner, has warned of the possible harm from women using drugs such as anabolic steroids. He felt that the evidence of his eyes led him to believe the East German lady swimmers had used them. Their "enormous" shoulder muscles, viewed by him on TV, could not have been produced, he claimed, by dumb-bell exercises.[67] The GDR keeps many of its recipes for Olympic success to itself, and explains the successes of its young ladies in terms of the changed status of women in its socialist society.

VI. *Women in sport*

The GDR owes a considerable part of its Olympic successes to its women. In 1956, they made up 21 per cent of the GDR's contribution to the all-German Olympic team. In 1972, they formed 23 per cent of the GDR's own team, but they won 50 per cent of the GDR's gold medals:[68]

Table 3.   GDR WOMEN'S CONTRIBUTION TO 1972 MUNICH
OLYMPIC RESULTS

Medals	GDR Total	GDR Women's Total
Gold	20	10
Silver	23	13
Bronze	23	9

On that occasion a Western sportswriter commented that the East German women

especially, were awesome in their ability albeit retaining a remarkable amount of femininity.[69]

In Montreal, their contribution to the prestige of their state was even more decisive: women made up 40 per cent of the GDR team (although women competed in only forty-nine of the 186 events—26 per cent); they won more than half the GDR's gold and silver medal total. The remarkable fact was that GDR women won more Olympic medals in Montreal than all other women put together. Among these GDR sports heroines was Renate Stecher, who won a silver medal in the 100m. at Montreal and

who has set half a dozen world records during a long career which has taken in European and Olympic sprint double crowns, not to mention the many relay gold medals.[70]

Rosemarie Ackermann won the gold in the high jump, was three times world record-breaker having made a dramatic comeback after failing at Munich. Johanna Schaller won the gold medal in the 100m. hurdles, which might well have been won by the remarkable Annelie Ehrhardt who did not qualify due to injury. Carola Domback made a brave effort to challenge the Soviet gymnasts on the pommelled horse, which, though not entirely successful, did result in a bronze medal. In the women's pentathlon the GDR girls Siegrun Siegl, Christine Laser and Burglinda Pollak won the first three places. In rowing, the East German women won medals in every event. But it was in swimming that they excelled most. And it is Kornelia Ender who will be best remembered with

her flawless style, based on a long, reaching stroke and tremendous flexibility; she developed the stamina and strength which brought her four gold medals in the Montreal Games—one more than any other female competitor in the history of the Olympics.[71]

These are just some of the successful women in sport in the German Democratic Republic. Many of them are the product of early selection, careful schooling and scientific training. But they are also the products of a society which, out of conviction and necessity, has tried to give women the opportunity to break out of the traditional boundaries, the old limitations on women's lives.

Of the full-time students at GDR universities in 1975, over 50 per cent were women—57,689 out of 103,089.[72] In 1973, 54·1 per cent of full-time students in all higher educational institutions in the GDR were women; in West Germany, by comparison, only 29·6 per cent were women.[73] Most school-teachers in the GDR are women, and, in 1974, 46 per cent of all doctors, 45 per cent of dentists, 61 per cent of pharmacists and 38·9 per cent of all professional judges were women.[74] A higher proportion of East German women in the relevant age groups go to work than do women in most other industrial states: in 1972, 51·9 per cent of women in West Germany between the ages of fifteen and sixty went out to work, while in the GDR the percentage was 80·9.[75] Nonetheless, women in the Democratic Republic, like women everywhere else, seem less interested in politics than their menfolk: only about 30 per cent of the members of the ruling SED are women, and there are few women in the highest echelons of the Party.

It is evident that the emancipation of women in the GDR has produced an impact on that state's sporting life, but concrete evidence is hard to come by. Official publications produce impressive statistics to show that year by year more women take part in sport in general, and competitive sport in particular. However, the writer has not seen any figures indicating a higher female rate of participation in the GDR than in the other states of Northern Europe or the other Warsaw Pact states. In the DTSB women are still underrepresented: of the 2·5 million members of that organisation in 1974, only 25 per cent were women. Even so, 43 per cent of the participants in the third sports competition for apprentices in 1973–4 were females.[76] Official publications also assert that women are prominent in the higher reaches of the DTSB.[77] Female participation in sport in the GDR is higher than in most Western and Eastern European states, and a larger choice for selectors may well explain in part the GDR's success in international women's sporting events.

VII. *Sport for everyone*

GDR publications are often responsible for the view of many in the West that the citizens of the GDR live according to spartan principles. Most of their time is evidently spent working, and when they are not working, they spend most of their free time working hard at either sport or politics. How accurate is this picture? First of all, let us look at the official sporting organisation, the DTSB. In 1973, 2·4 million East Germans were members, representing 14·3 per cent of the population of the GDR. Across the Elbe, the West German DSB had a membership of 9·8 millions or 16 per cent of the population.[78] The fact is that the great majority of East Germans do not take a regular and active part in sport. According to one authoritative East German investigator, in 1965 only 18 per cent of the population took part in sport more or less regularly. This figure included infants in kindergarten, children doing compulsory games in school, sport in the armed forces and police.[79] Herr Buggel, the investigator in question, found a lack of awareness among the public of any link between sport and health, and felt the authorities faced an ideological problem. The great majority in the 1960s claimed that they lacked time and opportunity, or admitted to lack of interest. Though there has been some increase in the numbers involved in sport since then, the picture has not changed radically. Interestingly, in 1968 a survey carried out among children between twelve and nineteen in Karl-Marx-Stadt, one of the GDR's fifteen administrative districts, revealed that about half of them did not pursue organised sport outside school hours. The largest single reason given for non-participation was that they had received bad marks in the compulsory sports sessions at school. This had turned them away from sport. Too much homework was the second, and too many jobs about the home was the third most frequent reason mentioned.[80] Other surveys have revealed similar attitudes. The search for champions in schools may well then have some adverse effect on interest and morale.

Of those people who engaged in sport in 1968, 48 per cent did so in the company of family or friends, and only 13 per cent did so within the framework of an official sports organisation.[81] In a survey of spare-time pursuits carried out in Karl-Marx-Stadt in 1968 among adults between eighteen and sixty-five, 37 per cent put sports or games first among *desired* leisure activities. But in the list of *actual* pursuits sport ranked eighth. Watching TV, followed by reading, were the most common pursuits, followed closely by discussion and handicrafts.

Another interesting aspect of recreation is the growing popularity of casual outdoor activities such as fishing. East German figures indicate that in 1975 fishing was the second most popular sport (after soccer) among members of the DTSB. Gymnastics was third, followed by athletics, skittles (a traditional German pastime) and handball.[82]

On the limited evidence available, it would appear that a great many people in the GDR are not as enthusiastic about sport as the authorities would like them to be, and that many who are interested see sport as merely a personal or family, casual recreational activity rather than an institutionalised one.

VIII. *Montreal and beyond*

The Montreal Games in 1976 produced triumphs for the GDR which must have been beyond the wildest dreams of all those responsible for the country's sport. For a country of under 17 millions to come second in terms of gold medals and beat the former world model in sport (with a population of over 200 millions), the mighty United States, is indeed a spectacular achievement. The GDR alone did better than the whole of Germany had done in the 1936 Games when the Germans were the winners. Table 4 indicates just how successful the GDR was compared with the other leading sporting nations.[83]

These figures for Montreal indicate that West Germany also did well in coming fourth. Both German states have benefited from the strong sports movement in Germany before the war, the German tradition of allying science and medicine to sport, and the tradition of state aid for sport. As in so many fields, both states have been involved in a grim rivalry with each other which is political in origin. This has also, in certain respects, proved an advantage to sport in the two German states.

A look at the GDR's Montreal Olympic team furnishes some more clues as to how this small state has produced so many successes. Of the 287 members of the East German squad, twenty-five came from the ASK, the armed forces sports club, fifty-eight from *Dynamo*, the club of the People's Police, twenty from the DHfK at Leipzig, and twenty-one from the club of state employees, *Einheit*—a total of 124.[84] Obviously, these are individuals who are given ample time to train, superior facilities, and are freed from financial insecurity. A look at some of the other GDR competitors further sheds light on official provision for sporting excellence: all the GDR's sailing team came from the club at Berlin-Grünau; the marksmen all originated from the

TABLE 4.   OLYMPIC RESULTS, MONTREAL 1976

Country	Gold	Silver	Bronze
USSR	47	43	35
GDR	40	25	25
USA	34	35	25
West Germany	10	12	17
Japan	9	6	10
Poland	8	6	11
Bulgaria	7	8	9
Cuba	6	4	3
Romania	4	9	14
Hungary	4	5	12
Finland	4	2	—
Sweden	4	1	—
Britain	3	5	5
Italy	2	7	4
Jugoslavia	2	3	3
France	2	2	5
Czechoslovakia	2	2	4
New Zealand	2	1	1

GST (six out of seven from Leipzig) or the People's Police club at Hoppengarten (as did the three judo entrants); the GDR's canoe squad was mainly from a club at Neubrandenburg; seven out of the twelve members of the Olympic volleyball team came from *SC Traktor* at Schwerin—a club for agricultural workers and technicians—and the majority of East German gymnasts competing at Montreal were from the chemical plant club at Halle. We are dealing here with the "secondment" of the best in certain fields to clubs which specialise in a few sports, the clubs being effectively closed to those who are just fairly good amateurs working in the chemical industry, agriculture, etc. Those bona fide employees who wish to pursue a sport on a casual basis may do so through the *Betriebssportgemeinschaften*—the workplace sports societies—rather than the specialist clubs.

The Winter Games at Innsbruck earlier in 1976 had also been dominated by the USSR and the GDR, with the USA coming third and Norway fourth. All the first eight successful countries had certain natural, climatic advantages over countries like Britain. But once again the East Germans did well to beat countries like West Germany (which came fifth), Austria and Switzerland. Even more than at Montreal, the GDR team was drawn from a very few specialists from an even smaller group of clubs. In fact, of the GDR ice-skating champions, five out of eight were *Dynamo* members, one was from the army club, one from *Einheit*, and one from *SC Traktor* based at the winter sports resort of Oberwiesenthal. Of the other winners, nine out of eleven were from the armed services club at the winter resort of Oberdorf, and again one was from *SC Traktor* Oberwiesenthal.[85] It is interesting to note that nearly forty doctors, coaches, officials, technicians and craftsmen were decorated for their work which had made this GDR success possible.

What of the future? There must be many in the sports movement and in the SED who would like to see the GDR take the final summit and become the most successful nation at the Moscow Olympics in 1980. Nonetheless, although the authorities will no doubt want to go on making supreme efforts, and are apparently taking some sensible measures[86] to pass on the skills acquired, there are limits to what they can do. Few know exactly how much they spend on sport; but in the future they may find that they will have to modify their expenditure. They also face the implications of a declining population with a very low reproduction rate.

At the conclusion of the Montreal Olympics, the President of the GDR Olympic Committee, Manfred Ewald, commented:

For the first time the athletes of the socialist countries have gained absolute ascendancy in the unofficial points' and medals' table. The sportsmen and women of the socialist countries—headed by the Soviet Union—received 54·5 per cent of the points.[87]

Herr Ewald praised the Soviet success as unprecedented in the Olympic Games.

But we as GDR athletes are also naturally happy that we have once again put up a good performance.

The East Germans had come second, and 159 of the 293 active members of the GDR team were returning home with medals. Herr Ewald recorded that the Canadian public had been fair to the GDR team, and made the significant point that

The GDR was very little known as a socialist state (in Canada). But I think that millions of Canadians now know better than before what ... the GDR means.[88]

It is, of course, impossible to measure the extent to which success in sport enhances a state's prestige or gives it a more positive image. However, although it would be wrong to see the GDR's sporting efforts *merely* in terms of internal and international image-building, there is no doubt that this has been an important consideration by GDR leaders. Where other channels have been closed, sport has been used to help attain a measure of recognition and prestige both at home and abroad for the young society that has grown up in the German Democratic Republic over the last thirty years.

NOTES

1. The GDR seems to have been discovered by Anglo-American academics in the 1960s and a number of books were published describing its politics and society: David Childs, *East Germany*, London, 1969; John Dornberg, *The Other Germany*, New York, 1968; Arthur Hanhardt, *The German Democratic Republic*, Baltimore, 1968; Peter Christian Ludz, *The German Democratic Republic from the Sixties to the Seventies*; Jean Edward Smith, *Germany beyond the Wall*, Boston, 1969; more recently, Kurt Sontheimer and Wilhelm Bleek, *The Government and Politics of East Germany*, London, 1975; John Starrels and Anita Mallinckrodt, *Politics in the German Democratic Republic*, New York, 1975.

2. I.e. before 1971.

3. See Martin Schnitzer on the East German economy in his *East and West Germany: A Comparative Economic Analysis*, New York, 1973.

4. Thomas M. Forster, *The East German Army*, London, 1967.

5. Arnd Krüger, *Sport und Politik von Turnvater Jahn zum Staatsamateur*, Hannover, 1975, p. 21.

6. *Geschichte der Deutschen Arbeiter Bewegung*, Band 1, Berlin, 1966, p. 438.

7. Krüger, op cit., p. 27.

8. Ibid, p. 33.

9. *Olympics' 76. Official British Olympic Association Preview*, London, 1976, p. 4.

10. Quoted in John Rickards Betts, *America's Sporting Heritage 1850–1950*, Reading, Mass., 1974, pp. 198–9.

11. See the comments of Alex Natan, "Sport and Politics" in John W. Loy, Jr. and G. S. Kenyon, *Sport, Culture and Society*, London, 1969.

12. Krüger, op. cit., p. 36.

13. Thomas Alexander and Beryl Parker, *The New Education in the German Republic*, London, 1930, p. 84.

14. Ibid., p. 84.

15. Ibid, p. 91.

16. Hermann Weber, *Die Wandlung des deutschen Kommunismus*, Frankfurt/M., 1969, p. 366.

17. Krüger, op. cit., p. 39.

18. Ibid, p. 87.

19. *Der Morgen*, 11 March 1976.

20. The German Democratic Republic was proclaimed in October 1949.

21. The number has varied as the trade unions have been re-organised.

22. These paralleled the Soviet sports societies *Shakhtyor*, *Lokomotiv*, *Spartak* and *Dinamo* respectively.

23. The text is given in Siegfried Baske, Martha Engelbert, *Zwei Jahrzehnte Bildungspolitik in der Sowjetzone Deutschlands*, vol. 1, Berlin, 1966.

24. Baske and Engelbert, op. cit., pp. 156–7.

25. In theory there are five political parties in the GDR. In practice, already by 1950 the other four were fundamentally committed to the SED's policies, severely restricted in their spheres of operation, and were rapidly becoming mere "echoes" of the ruling SED.

26. The translation is the author's own.

27. The author paid his first visit to the GDR at this time.

28. Rudolf Kabel, *Die Militarisierung der Sowjetischen Besatsungszone Deutschlands—Bericht und Dokumentation*, Bonn, 1966, p. 46.

29. Forster, op. cit., contains sections on the GST and the FDJ.

30. Even under the DSA there had been certain specialist associations.

31. *Sport in der Deutschen Demokratischen Republik*, published by the Friedrich-Ebert-Stiftung, Bonn, 1975, pp. 12–13.

32. Krüger, op. cit., p. 110.

33. Rudi Reichert (born 1922), after wartime service in the Wehrmacht, joined the FDJ, becoming its sports organiser in Mecklenberg. He was put in charge of the DSA when that body was formed and became a member of the State Committee in 1952. In 1957 Reichert was made President of the new sports organisation, DTSB. Between 1958 and 1963 he was a member of the Central Committee of the SED and of the DDR parliament.

34. For the text of his remarks see *Protokoll des V. Parteitages der Sozialistichen Einheitspartei Deutschlands, Berlin*, 1959, vol. 2, pp. 1254–9.

35. Manfred Ewald (born 1926), the son of a tailor, was a youth leader in Stettin at eighteen and then served briefly in the war ending it as a POW of the Soviet Union. He worked his way up through the FDJ, joining the DSA in 1948. Between 1952 and 1960 he was Chairman of the State Committee, becoming President of the DTSB in 1961. Highly decorated for his services to sport and politics, he was promoted to membership of the Central Committee of the SED in 1963 and, in the same year, was elected to the GDR parliament.

36. Krüger, op. cit., p. 142.

37. Wilhelm Schneller, *Die Deutsche Demokratische Schule*, Berlin, 1955, p. 7.

38. Dietrich Martin, *Schulsport in Deutschland*, Schorndorf, 1972, p. 79.

39. It is interesting that Schneller hardly mentions physical education in his official East German account of schools.

40. *SBZ von A–Z*, edited by Günter Fischbach, Bonn, 1966, p. 146.

41. *Statistiches Jahrbuch der DDR 1957*, pp. 125–6.

42. Martin, op. cit., p. 90.

43. There were exceptions, of course, for physically-handicapped children.

44. Mina J. Moore-Rinvolucri, *Education in East Germany*, Newton Abbot, 1973, p. 53.

45. Baske and Engelbert, op. cit., vol. II, 1959–65, pp. 305–7.

46. Baske and Engelbert, op. cit., pp. 262–3.

47. Here one is speaking relatively, for emphasis on GST activities remained throughout the 1950s.

48. Apart from comments from individual East Germans, the fact that FDJ and NVA officials sit on university entrance-commissions would make would-be students think twice about not taking part.

49. *Statistiches Jahrbuch der DDR 1963*, pp. 439, 480.

50. Manfred Ewald reported in *Theorie und Praxis der Körperkultur*, August, 1976, p. 624.

51. Dieter Voigt, *Soziologie in der DDR*, Cologne, 1975, p. 41. He is quoting the Deputy Defence Minister of the GDR.

52. *Statistiches Jahrbuch der DDR 1969*, pp. 373, 405.

53. Voigt, op. cit., p. 41.

54. These figures are in Voigt, op. cit., p. 67; he has taken them from the respective statistical yearbooks of the two German states.

55. *Sport in der Deutschen Demokratischen Republik*, op. cit., p. 22.

56. *Education in the German Democratic Republic*, Leipzig, 1962, p. 37.

57. *Sport in . . .* , op. cit., p. 37.

58. *Unser Bildungssystem—wichtiger Schritt auf dem Wege zur gebildeten Nation*, Staatsverlag der DDR, 1965, p. 101.

59. *DDR Handbuch*, edited by Peter Christian Ludz, Cologne, 1975, pp. 805-6.

60. *Deutsche Hochschule für Körperkultur Leipzig—DDR*, Dresden, 1975, This is the official handbook of the University.

61. David Johnston, "East Germany—Distinctive Features", in Edmund J. King (ed.), *Communist Education*, London, 1963, pp. 208-9.

62. *Theorie und Praxis der Körperkultur*, October 1976, p. 747. Jochen Heimrich, Günter Hafenberg, "25 Jahre Sportunterricht an den Universitäten, Hochund Fachschulen der DDR".

63. Heimrich, Hafenberg, op. cit., p. 749.

64. Ibid., p. 748.

65. Willi Knecht, "Massensport als Ausdruck des sozialistischen Leistungsethos," *Deutschland Archiv*, Bonn, 1/1977.

66. James Coote, *Olympic Report 76*, London, 1976, pp. 53-4.

67. "Herkules aus der Retorte", *Die Zeit* (Hamburg), 13 August 1976. On the other hand, the distinguished Nobel Peace Prize-winner and former British Olympic champion, Philip Noel-Baker, who has visited GDR sports organisations, has told the writer that he did not feel that the East Germans would use anabolic steroids.

68. *Women in the GDR. Facts and Figures*, Dresden, 1975, p. 31; *Sport in der Deutschen Demokratischen Republik*, op. cit., p. 14.

69. Coote, *History of the Olympics*, op. cit., p. 133.

70. *Olympic Report 76*, op. cit., p. 43.

71. Ibid. p. 52.

72. *Statistiches Taschenbuch der DDR 1976*, p. 127.

73. *Zahlenspiegel Ein Vergleich Bundesrepublik Deutschland/Deutsche Demokratische Republik*, Gesamtdeutsches Institut, Bonn, 1974, p. 39.

74. *Women in . . .* op. cit., p. 49.

75. *Zahlenspiegel . . .* , op. cit., p. 14.

76. *Women in. . . .*, op. cit., p. 30.

77. Heidi Biersted, Margitta Gummel, "Sportliche Betätigung und Emanzipation der Frau", *Theorie und Praxis der Körperkultur*, 1976, No. 11, p. 845. They mention that twenty-six women are on the executive of the DTSB, but they do not say out of how many.

78. Voigt, op. cit., p. 67. He has taken the figures from the respective yearbooks.

79. Ibid, p. 86. He is quoting E. Buggel, *Wissenschaftliche Zeitschrift der Karl-Marx-Universität*, Leipzig, 1963, vol. I, No. 12. Buggel is now Vice-President of the DTSB.

80. Ibid, p. 88.

81. Ibid, p. 60.

82. *Statistisches Taschenbuch der Deutschen Demokratischen Republik*, 1976, p. 134.

83. Taken from *Frankfurter Allgemeine Zeitung*, 3 August 1976, and *Neues Deutschland*, 3 March 1976.

84. *Der Morgen*, 22 June 1976.

85. *Der Morgen*, 26 March 1976.

86. A laudable aspect of GDR sport is the way athletes are encouraged to prepare for careers later and to pass on their expertise. Thus, ex-champions Ulla Donath, Manfred Matuschewski and Renate Dannhauer have all found jobs in sport. See *Der Morgen*, 1 Sept. 1974; 26 June 1976; 21 Feb. 1976.

87. *Der Morgen*, 3 August 1976. For a West German view of GDR sport, see Christian Graf von Krockow, "Die Olympische Grossmacht GDR", *Die Zeit*, 16 July 1976; Willi Knecht, *Deutschland Archiv*, January, 1977.

88. *Der Morgen*, loc. cit.

Roy A. Clumpner and Brian B. Pendleton

THE PEOPLE'S REPUBLIC OF CHINA

PERSONAL NOTES

Roy Clumpner, a graduate of the University of Alberta, Edmonton, teaches international and comparative physical education at Western Washington University. Dr. Clumpner has travelled extensively and, during the past ten years, has lived in Japan, the Federal Republic of Germany, Canada and the United States. He is the present Secretary of the International Relations Council of the American Alliance for Health, Physical Education and Recreation. His most recent publication focused on American government involvement in sport.

Brian Pendleton is a member of the faculty at Vancouver Community College where he teaches physical education and Chinese politics. A graduate of the University of Alberta, Edmonton, he has, in addition to visiting China on several occasions, studied and lectured on sport in the Soviet Union and the German Democratic Republic. Among his current research projects is a study of Chinese international sport and the question of recognition in the Olympic movement.

CONTENTS

Introduction

Our Western perspective has given rise to a number of misconceptions regarding China which must be considered at the outset if we are to avoid what Mao Zedong* described as "Looking at the flowers from horseback"; we must instead dismount, analyse and investigate more closely. With over a 4,000-year history, China has evolved into a multiethnic state of over 800 million people who inhabit the world's third largest country. The People's Republic of China consists of twenty-two provinces, five autonomous regions and three municipal districts in which 80 per cent of the population is engaged in agriculture. Since 1949, government and state organisations have been unified under the leadership of the Chinese Communist Party whose membership now exceeds 35 million.

(i) Chinese sport: a rich heritage

Chinese interest in sport is not new. In fact, Chinese involvement in sport, games and health exercises pre-dates that of most cultures. Literary and artistic evidence suggests that the Chinese people have had a long-standing awareness of sport and, for a small section of the population, a history of active participation in sport over the centuries. As in many cultures, such daily activities as fishing, hunting and swimming that were required for survival and subsistence grew into leisure pursuits for the nobility and the privileged classes. In addition to these active forms of recreation, table games such as *weigi* (Chinese "go") and *xiangqi* (Chinese chess), dancing and gambling have deep roots in Chinese culture.[1] Han and Tang dynasty stone carvings and earthenware artifacts have been discovered which depict dancing, musical and gambling activities of the ruling classes.[2] The acrobats and jugglers

---

* Mao Zedong (Mao Tse-tung). The accepted method of romanisation currently used in the People's Republic, *hanyu pinyin*, will be used throughout this study. Certain Chinese names and terms (e.g. Mao Tse-tung, Chiang Kai-shek, Kung Fu) have become extremely familiar in the traditional Wade-Giles romanisation, and such will appear in brackets following the *pinyin* romanisation.

who today excite both Chinese and foreign audiences carry on the rich cultural heritage of their ancestors.

Historians have also noted the presence throughout Chinese history of various ball games, the forerunners of modern football, polo and golf. For example, football (*zuqiu*) was known in China during the fourth century BC and, prior to the appearance of an inflatable ball, was played with a round leather object stuffed with hair and feathers. Handling of the ball was not permitted and a referee was present to control the play.[3] Han and Tang dynasty illustrations depict the game being played between two teams within defined boundaries and later drawings detail the form and construction of the goal area.[4] In a fifteenth century painting the emperor is seen watching not only football and archery, but also a polo match.[5]

In addition to these sporting contests, references have been made to a variety of other activities ranging from kite flying and shuttlecock (badminton) to swimming in the southern regions and ice activities in the north (a form of ice hockey with formal rules is said to have existed in the north).[6]

It is, however, from the military arts of ancient China that much may be gleaned regarding early sporting activity. The concern with military affairs has created a cultural tradition which continues to flourish today. Thus, the term *wushu* embraces the martial arts of archery, fencing, wrestling, boxing, and a variety of activities involving clubs, spears and swords.[7]

One *wushu* activity which has continued in popularity in present-day China is Chinese boxing of which two styles have evolved: the inner school and the outer school.[8] Of the many forms of the inner school, taijiquan (*taichichuan*) is the most widely practised. It emphasises body movements using tactics incorporating defence and endurance, and is characterised by slow body-movements with an emphasis on the coordination of breathing and movement. The outer school is best known through the Shaolin system introduced in the sixth Century by monks of the Shaolin monastery in Honan province, as a daily exercise to improve their health. It later became a means of self-defence with numerous movements which stressed quickness, kicking and striking followed by a retreating acrobatic bound. The recently popularised *gong fu* (Kung Fu) styles owe their beginnings to the Shaolin forms, although *gong fu* is, technically, a generic term for all forms of exercise and not a particular style in itself.

Inherent in both the above-mentioned schools of boxing was an awareness of the health and fitness components of exercise and sport. This was especially true of Shaolin which stressed regular habits, self-discipline, a vegetable diet, sexual restraint and prohibition of stimulants.

Recent archaeological discoveries provide evidence of the existence of systematic exercise programmes over 2,000 years ago. Of a series of over forty tomb drawings unearthed near Changsha during excavations, thirty-one were preserved in a condition which permitted interpretation of the figures and translation of the accompanying script. Three distinct categories of movement were evident: breathing exercises, exercises of the arms and legs, and exercises with balls and sticks.[9]

The Chinese concept of the body was greatly influenced during the Han dynasty (206 BC–AD 220) when the doctrines of Confucianism, Taoism and Buddhism gained official approval. For the next 2,000 years they succeeded in pushing physical culture into the background at the expense of the mind. Buddhism and Taoism were both religions intended for the masses; they taught the uselessness of worldly striving, and held out hope for the downtrodden through salvation after death. Confucianism on the other hand was an aristocratic, conservative, politico-moral doctrinaire system which stressed the necessity of each individual dutifully performing his or her obligation to others. Morality and social order were prized, with past tradition becoming a "god" before whom all were to bow. Therefore, from Buddhism, Taoism and Confucianism there developed a distain for physical activity and in its place was stressed the quiet, studious, contemplative life. It was against these anti-physical attitudes that the proponents of physical culture had to contend. By the second half of the nineteenth century, some of these barriers were being removed and two divergent approaches to physical culture emerged.

Gradually, as China moved closer to the twentieth century the concept of good health through exercise reached more and more Chinese, largely due to the influence of Westerners whose personal habits often served as an example and whose exercise programmes, partly conducted by the YMCA, gained increasing acceptance. Westerners also contributed, albeit indirectly, to the fitness movement when it became more and more evident that China would only rid herself of occupying forces through physical force; thus, the concept of building up the people's health to break the chains of imperialism became popular.

(ii) *Beginnings of modern sport*

Through contact with the West, China was introduced to the idea of including formal exercise programme in military training. As a result, such a programme was introduced to Nanjing (Nanking) Military College which was established in 1875, the Tianjin (Tientsin) Naval Academy (1881) and the Hubei Military Academy (1895). The programme included formal military-type exercises and gymnastics under the direction of a Japanese or a German instructor. This exercise programme was later to be adopted by the government schools in 1905, when legislation ruled that three to five hours of exercise had to be introduced initially for elementary schools and later for middle and lower normal schools as well as for lower agriculture schools.

A second exposure to modern physical culture was afforded the Chinese through Western sport first as a recreational pastime and later as physical education. It was at missionary schools and the YMCA where such organised Western sports as baseball, basketball, table tennis, athletics, volleyball and gymnastics were first introduced.[10] As early as 1890, athletics made its appearance at St. John's University in Shanghai, followed by basketball in 1896 at the Tianjin YMCA. The YMCA played an important role not only in the development of physical education, but also in laying the foundations of China's first national athletics association. In addition, it ran an extensive training programme for its own sports directors. In 1918, the YMCA School of Physical Education at the Association College of China began a two-year course for physical training instructors and a four-year course for directors. These courses, however, did have their limitations, as did those which the government tried to implement. Although restrictions were often placed on Chinese wishing to enroll in YMCA courses, in the early part of the century the government turned increasingly to the YMCA for both in-service training and the organisation of physical education departments in government schools. Eventually, the YMCA influence diminished, largely because of growing hostility towards foreigners in the mid-1920s and lack of sound leadership and manpower in the movement itself.

Paralleling these changes was a series of provincial and national championships pioneered by the YMCA under the leadership of Dr. Max J. Exner, the first National YMCA Director in Shanghai. Shortly after, Chinese athletes entered a major international competition for the first time: the Far Eastern Championship Games (FECG) in 1913; the Games survived until the early years of the Sino-Japanese conflict just before the outbreak of World War II.

The significance of these Games is difficult to assess. At least, they did encourage participation in sport and indirectly caused the government to promulgate laws on physical education and to convene conferences; they may also have contributed to enhancing national pride among the Chinese.

Another influence on the development of sport and physical education in China early in the twentieth century was the consolidation of a national Chinese government. The period from October 1928 until September 1949 marked the era of official rule by the Nationalist

Government of Jiang Jie shi (Chiang Kai-shek) and the Guomindang (Kuomintang) Party, although at no time during the two decades could it be said that China was unified under a central, stable government. The political climate was first one of limited civil war, then of a war of resistance to the Japanese, and finally of an all-out civil war which eventually saw Jiang's retreat to the island-province of Taiwan in the face of the advance of the Communist armies.

The social, economic and political conditions of the 1930s and 1940s were hardly conducive to a planned development of sport. Nevertheless, the government's record of accomplishments was not totally blank. A National Physical Education Law was enacted in 1929 and remained in effect, in theory if not in practice, for twenty years. As a result of the Law, the Ministry of Education stipulated that physical education was to have a weekly time allotment of two to three hours per week at all levels of schooling and that new national curricula should include daily morning exercise and 30–50 minutes of after-school physical recreation and military training.[11]

Further, the first national physical education conference was convened in 1932 and the government assumed responsibility, through the China National Amateur Athletics Federation (CNAAF), for the sponsorship of the 4th to 10th National Athletics Championships. In response to the demands of a nation at war, sport and physical education underwent a "militarisation" with increased emphasis on Boy Scout and Girl Guide organisations, the promotion of gliding associations and the construction of parachute towers in the wartime capital of Zhongqing (Chungking).

Internationally, China joined the International Olympic Committee in the mid-1920s and sent athletes to the Olympic Games of 1932, 1936 and 1948. Their performance, understandably, was mediocre.

In retrospect, it is difficult to analyse the effects of the programmes developed under the Guomindang as far as physical culture is concerned. One must be constantly aware of the internal and international conflicts that existed at this time. It should be acknowledged, nonetheless, that attempts were made to introduce school physical education and to initiate national sporting events. Despite these measures, by the time the Communist Party came to power in 1949, the vast majority of Chinese had never stepped into a classroom, much less participated in physical education or sport. The observations made by a foreign journalist on the plight of the Chinese people at the turn of the century were still applicable on the eve of liberation.

To the poor, who form an immense majority of the population, life is a never ending struggle against starvation. They rise at dawn and work until dark, have no Sunday or other rest days in the year . . . With them half a day of idleness means half a day of hunger, and they appear to lack both opportunity and capacity for what is called social enjoyment.[12]

I. Evolution of sport in the New China

On 1 October 1949, Mao Zedong stood on the rostrum overlooking Tiananmen Square in Peking and proclaimed the establishment of the People's Republic of China. Forming the central ideological basis for Mao and the people of new China at that time, and continuing to guide the country to the present, has been Mao's interpretation of Marxism and his application of dialectics to the concept of "contradiction". To the Chinese, contradictions are seen as being a universal and permanent feature of all social life, and not phenomena unique only to Chinese society. Therefore, conflict and change in dialectical analysis is considered to be natural, whereas stability and continuity, so much emphasised in the West, are seen as only temporary states. Failure to grasp this essential difference in philosophical outlook is a primary cause of misunderstanding by Western observers and analysts in studying the Chinese polity.

Thus, it should come as no surprise that "continuing revolution" (*jixu geming*) is an enduring feature of all social and political life, including the practice of sport, in People's China. Throughout the short history of the People's Republic then, the concept of contradiction has manifested itself in one recurring theme—class struggle—and it was from this perspective that in 1966 the Great Proletarian Cultural Revolution took place with the prime aim of creating a "new socialist man".

While the emphasis on contradictions is unique to the People's Republic, China's political culture shares three essential elements with all other societies: ideology, leadership and implementation. By analysing the values and beliefs of society (ideology), the guidance and direction (leadership) and the delivery system (implementation), the development and conduct of physical culture in the People's Republic can better be understood.

The Chinese view "physical culture" as an all-encompassing term including: (1) the school curriculum—physical education (*tiyu*), (2) competitions and ball games—sports and athletics (*yundong*), and (3) exercise programme—fitness and conditioning (*duanlian*). Although the distinctions are important and should be noted, the generic term physical culture will be used throughout this chapter.

(i) Ideology

In its broadest and most practical sense, the ideological and philosophical foundation of modern China is to be found in the slogan "Serve the people" (*wei renmin fuwu*). Physical culture is no exception:

Culture and education, literature and art, physical education, health work and scientific research must all serve proletarian politics, serve the workers, peasants and soldiers, and be combined with productive labour.[13]

This principle has resulted in numerous similar references to physical culture in Party documents since 1950. For example, in "The Common Programme", China's blueprint for action just prior to formulation of its first constitution, emphasis was placed on the need to promote national sports, expand public health and medical work, and safeguard the health of mothers, infants and children.[14] Similar reference was made in the first Constitution to the notion that the state should pay special attention to the physical and mental development of young people.[15]

The concept "Serve the people" has several meanings. It can refer to the idea of physical culture serving the people by encouraging them to become physically healthy; it can serve the people by enabling them to become physically fit for higher productivity and it can better prepare them for defence of their country. Over the years these functions, have undergone changes in emphasis depending on the demands of the times. No single specific purpose seems to have overridden the others. In the same vein is another ideological principle expressed in the slogan "Friendship first, competition second" (youyi diyi bisai dier). This concept was widely publicised both inside and outside China in the 1970s whenever sporting competitions took place among the Chinese themselves or with countries considered as friends. Basically, this motto has acted as an internal unifying force and has presented a picture in which others may see socialism's fraternal concepts in practice. Both these concepts—"Serve the people" and "Friendship first, competition second"—continue to influence physical culture.

(ii) Leadership

Mao's first written acknowledgement of the importance of physical activity appeared during his early years as a revolutionary. In an article written in 1917 and entitled "A Study of Physical Culture",[16] he emphasised the need for the people to become physically strong and he proposed a series of regular exercises designed for general overall body development and conditioning.

Mao's official endorsement of physical culture had to wait until after the revolution. This took place on 10 June 1952, when he called upon the Chinese people to "promote physical culture and sport, and build up the people's health." This directive focused the attention of the Chinese people on the importance of physical culture which has continued to be an important aspect of daily life in China today. Each year this landmark is celebrated throughout the country in a

commemorative physical culture day, marked by exhibitions, pro-
cessions, displays, and full coverage in the national press.

Mao reinforced his 1952 directive and gave further support to physical culture in 1953 when he declared,

New China must care for her young and show concern for the growth of the
younger generation. Young people have to study and work, but they are at the
age of physical growth. Therefore, full attention must be paid both to their
work and study and to their recreation, sport and rest.[17]

Since then, similar references by Mao to physical culture have appeared, all of which persist in their encouragement:

Our educational policy must enable everyone who receives an education to
develop morally, intellectually and physically, and become a worker with both
socialist consciousness and culture.[18]

Wherever feasible, physical culture and sports of all kinds should be encouraged,
such as physical exercises, ball games, running, mountain climbing, swimming
and traditional Chinese boxing.[19]

Of equal impact in the promotion of physical culture was the personal
example set by Mao. In his later years he became overweight and was
often pictured as a heavy smoker; however, his involvement in physical
activity and sport provided the Chinese people with a model they could
emulate. Although his personal enjoyment of physical activities such
as hiking and swimming during his youth was well publicised, it was
his personal involvement and example after 1949 which gave direction
and guidance to the Chinese people. On several occasions his involvement coincided with campaigns designed to motivate and mobilise
the masses for political action. In 1956, when Mao on three separate
occasions swam across the Yangtze River at Wuhan, and in 1969,
when he swam in the Ming Tombs Reservoirs, national emphasis placed
on swimming reflected the state's concern for fitness and defence, and
served to reinforce ideological training.

This combination of politics and sporting prowess reached a peak in
1966 when Mao again entered the water at Wuhan to symbolise his
strength and perseverance against those who were mounting attacks
on his policies in the then unfolding Cultural Revolution. The
implications and significance attached to this day (16 July), which is
commemorated nationally, go far beyond the physical act of swimming. In subsequent years a parallel was to be made between the effort
needed to learn swimming and to continue the political revolution.
In a front-page article entitled "Advance in the Teeth of Storms and
Waves," the People's Daily likened the on-going class struggle to the
challenge of swimming.

Freedom consists in knowledge of necessity and transformation of the objective world. It is easier to learn swimming by mastering the laws in the course of swimming. This is also true in carrying out class struggle.[20]

Although physical culture here was used for political purposes, nevertheless the 1976 commemoration of this swim did encourage an interest in swimming. Following Mao's example, mass swimming activities took place throughout the country. In Wuhan, for example, 12,000 local swimmers are said to have joined in the cross-Yangtze swim.

In addition to mass media coverage of these swimming spectacles, other methods were used to enhance the popularity of swimming. A series of three postage stamps was issued commemorating the 1966 swim; Mao's 1965 poem "Swimming" was given prominence, and numerous paintings, songs and poems composed by ordinary men and women on the topic were circulated in newspapers along with photographs of the historic swim.

This example of Mao promoting swimming is not to suggest that he provided the *sole* leadership and inspiration for physical culture; rather that his personal example was catalytic to a degree unprecedented in history. True, other aspects, such as the formal institutional leadership which directs the day-to-day sports operations and the programmes associated with officials (see below), have influenced and continue to influence the direction and scope of physical culture in China. However, no one leader ever had such an impact on physical culture in China as had Mao Zedong.

(iii) *Implementation*

One of the most persistent problems which the Chinese faced throughout their history was the lack of a communication system. With the establishment of a unified government, this problem has diminished somewhat and information is readily available today to the public throughout China. All forms of the media are used to promote physical culture. The People's Sports Publishing House (*Renmin Tiyu Chubanshe*) serves as the main centre for the preparation and distribution of printed materials. It is from here that such periodicals as the monthly *New Physical Culture* (*Xin Tiyu*) and the twice-weekly *Physical Culture News* (*Tiyu Bao*) are published. Similarly, the Publishing House has issued both Chinese and English language editions of a ninety-five-page pictorial entitled *Sports in China* (*Zhongguo Tiyu*). In addition to these items, the Publishing House makes available in its bookstores throughout the country numerous guidebooks, pamphlets, instructional posters, novels and illustrated books for children pertaining to physical culture.

Besides printed materials, other forms of mass media are used extensively. In co-operation with the China Record Company, records have been produced to accompany the mass exercise programme. Also, the military band of the People's Liberation Army has recorded "March of the Sportsmen" (*Yundongyuan Jinxinggu*) for use at the opening and closing ceremonies of all athletic events. Extensive use is also made of television, radio and film studios in providing coverage of major sporting events. Most noteworthy in this regard is the contribution made by the Central Newsreels and Documentary Film Studio of Peking in producing the full-length feature, "The 7th Asian Games", and a documentary on the Third National Games entitled "Ode to the Red Flag". Finally, the Ministry of Posts and Telecommunications regularly issues colourful postage stamps depicting various sporting scenes, past and future events, and sporting philosophies such as "Friendship first, competition second".

The second method used to promote physical culture has been to train personnel. To this end, the Chinese government moved quickly after liberation to offer short-term training courses for those desiring such training. Today, post-middle school training offers two formal routes for those desiring to become teachers or coaches of physical culture. One route is through an established physical culture institute and the other is through a physical culture department in a teacher training college, otherwise known as a normal school. Originally, in the 1950s and 1960s, the physical culture institutes were designed to train teachers, coaches, researchers, officials and administrators as well as top athletes, while the physical culture department of a normal school was essentially for the training of teachers for primary and middle schools. In the latter, emphasis was placed on teaching methods and techniques rather than on specialisation in one or more areas of physical culture. With the dust finally settling in the aftermath of the Cultural Revolution and Mao's departure, it is still difficult to tell whether or not any major changes have occurred in this system. While much of what had been happening in educational methodology has been changed, the "system" appears to have remained intact.

There is a third, indirect method of training personnel which is outside the normal educational channels. Generally this is done in one of two ways. The first is through the "spare time sports schools" which were established in 1955 to train future international athletes. Athletes who attend such schools are encouraged to become proficient and, in addition, to return to their schools and neighbourhoods to share their knowledge, skills and experiences with others. This practice is often referred to as "each-one-teach-one" and serves two purposes: first, those who are not able to attend the schools can receive training from the spare-time school student-athletes: and secondly, the young athletes in the school receive ideological training in the movement to have sport serve proletarian politics. A second way in which training is received outside the formal channels occurs when, for example, interested factory workers who wish to train in one sport are sent to attend clinics and workshops on the understanding that they will return and train factory teams and their fellow-workers. Again the principle is that one shares one's expertise and experience with others rather than merely increasing personal ability and knowledge.

By means of these programmes the Chinese are able to offer training in several aspects of sport and physical culture. While most of the concepts employed have not been original (e.g. spare-time schools), the Chinese have been successful in adapting traditional training systems and models to their own needs, thus making the implementation of the entire programme more feasible.

Finally, a major factor in the implementation of physical culture in China has been the evolution of a formal organisational structure responsible for the planning, coordinating and directing of programmes and services. It is not surprising that soon after liberation the government should establish state organisations to oversee sport and physical culture. Initially influenced by the Soviet method of organisation, the Chinese system has enabled physical culture to progress at a steady pace towards the interrelated goals of mass participation and the raising of standards at national and international levels.

II. Organisation and administration

(i) National level

Two major national organs exist for the promotion of physical culture and sport in China. The Physical Culture and Sports Commission (Tiyu Yundong Weiyuanhui), established on 15 November 1952 as a central government ministry with offices in Peking, is responsible for policy setting, financial planning, personnel training and propaganda (public relations); it acts as a liaison with other government ministries such as Education, Public Health and National Defence. Representatives of the PCSC work in each of the provinces and provide, to use a Chinese expression, "vocational guidance" in disseminating information to and soliciting input from the local areas.

The second body which plays a role in physical culture is the All-China Sports Federation (Zhonghua Quanguo Tiyu Zonghui). Created in October 1949, the ACSF is responsible for the organisation of mass sport, fitness and recreation; the coordination of local, national and international competitions; and the provision of support services including the recruitment and training of coaches and officials, and scientific research and testing. These latter responsibilities are co-ordinated with the efforts of local educational institutions and departments. In addition, the ACSF serves as the "Chinese Olympic Committee" to which individual national sports governing bodies, such as the Football Association (*Zuqiu Xiehui*), are affiliated.

Figure 1 depicts the relationship of the ACSF as a "mass organisation" to the PCSC as the government ministry.

Notwithstanding the structurally subordinate role of the ACSF, this body is clearly the major provider of sport throughout the country. Sport and physical culture personnel serving in factories, offices, commercial enterprises, communes, national minority areas, the People's Liberation Army and schools and colleges all maintain close ties with officials of the All-China Sports Federation. In addition, all major competitions are arranged in consultation with ACSF personnel and international liaison is carried on through these offices.

(ii) *Provincial and local levels*

Although both organs are represented at provincial and local levels, no uniform pattern exists in all areas of the country. Figure 2 illustrates a representative provincial organisational structure.

Under the leadership of this particular Revolutionary Committee, based in the provincial capital of Sian, a twelve-member Physical Culture Committee coordinates the work of a general office which had, in 1976, five sections:[21] 1. mass sport; 2. training of personnel; 3. political affairs; 4. military training; 5. planning and financial affairs.

Representatives from the Women's Federation, the trade unions, the Young Communist League and the Peasants' Association work closely with the staff of the Physical Culture Committee in identifying interests and needs, designing programmes, and mobilising resources for the communities, groups and individuals concerned.

The close interaction between these various units and governmental organs often tends to blur the lines of designated responsibility and authority and, thus, in Western terms, makes definitive analysis difficult. For the Chinese, however, the system *does* work, and provides opportunities for individuals and groups to take part in sport and recreational activities on a regular basis.

(iii) *Leading officials*

One of the major factors in China's continuing progress in physical culture since 1949 has been the availability of knowledgeable and experienced personnel at all levels. In addition to the continuity of service over many years, several leading personalities have concurrently held positions in both the PCSC and the ACSF. Such dual appointments have provided the necessary linkage between the policy-setting and the implementing bodies in the Chinese system. At the State Council level

Fig. 1. ORGANISATIONAL RELATIONSHIPS IN CHINESE SPORT

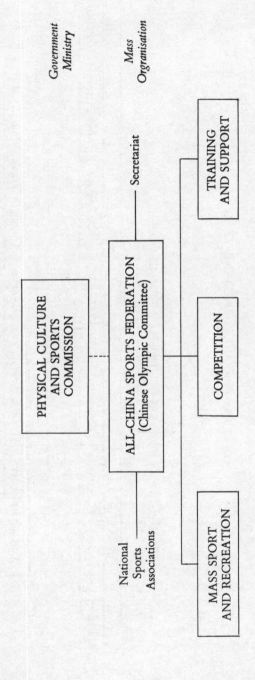

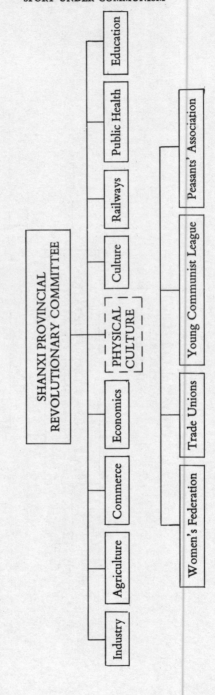

Fig. 2. PROVINCIAL ORGANISATION (SHANXI)

only three individuals have served as Minister of the PCSC: He Long (1954–66), Wang Meng (1971–5 and from 1977), and Zhuang Ze-dong (1975–7).[22] No ministerial appointment was made during the Cultural Revolution when the Commission was placed under the control of the General Political Department of the People's Liberation Army. Physical culture interests have also been well-represented over the years within the Chinese Communist Party. Most recently, at the 11th Party Congress in August 1977, two individuals were elected to full membership in the Central Committee—Minister Wang Meng and Li Da, a former Chairman of the Military Sports Association and a past Vice-Chairman of the PCSC.[23]

III. The Conduct of sport and physical culture

(i) Exercise, fitness and recreation

One of the foundations for China's sport and physical culture is the mass exercise and fitness programmes which have been promoted since 1951. As mentioned previously, the desire to create a Chinese citizenry physically fit enough to throw off the chains of colonialism was espoused by Mao Zedong as early as 1917. Mao developed a programme of six exercises to be practised twice a day (mornings and evenings); its implementation on a countrywide scale did not take place until late 1951 when the country's first set of calisthenics was issued by the Preparatory Committee of the State Commission on Physical Culture and Sport. Four sets of calisthenics were introduced, with subsequent changes and alterations made in 1954, 1957 and 1963. From available accounts, however, the exercises were too long and difficult to be learned by the peasants, workers and soldiers.[24]

In 1969, a group of specialists began to prepare a new set of calisthenic exercises. The group reported that it had found that persons engaged in both manual and office jobs most often worked in a body position in which they were bent forward. Certain parts of their bodies were used a great deal while the rest of the body made little movement. As a result, a new set of exercises was designed to include more back movements, chest extension and stretching of the arm and shoulder muscles. In addition, a more lively piece of musical accompaniment was composed.

In 1971, the new calisthenic programme was introduced and remains in force today. Basically, the five-minute exercise entails eight body movements, beginning and ending with marching on the spot. Official Chinese news reports present a picture of universal participation:

Exercises take place early every morning and at the start of fifteen-minute work breaks in morning and afternoon. It is mass-exercise time and in nearly every place in China one can see workers, commune members, army-men, office personnel and school children turning out.[25]

In actuality, the degree of participation varies with the groups concerned and the location. Widespread involvement in the programme is highest in the elementary and secondary schools and the military, is less successful at factories and offices in urban areas and is lowest on the rural communes where people have obviously less need for such exercise since physical labour is part of their daily life.

More popular in factories would seem to be exercises designed specifically for workers of different trades. This is said to have begun in 1973 when teachers and students from the Peking Physical Culture Institute visited various manufacturing centres in Peking to find out what types of exercises were needed by the workers. From this they created seven sets of three-to-five minute exercises aimed at relieving fatigue and strain when certain parts of the body were used continuously, and at preventing industrial diseases.[26] Another example of specific exercises are those involving massaging routines designed to relieve tension and fatigue, and to strengthen the eye muscles. In both instances, exercises were created in response to specific needs.

Finally, linking all sectors of society in promoting exercise and fitness are the Standards of the National Physical Training Programme which were revised most recently in 1975. Modelled on the Soviet "Ready for Labour and Defence" programme of 1931, and based on the conditions in China at the time of liberation in 1949, these fitness tests were devised in the early 1950s. Following a period of initial experimentation and evaluation, the programme was finally ratified by the Chinese Government in May 1954. In response to more extensive, nationwide experience, the standards underwent significant revision in 1958: the original nine events were reduced to five for youngsters and six for adults; the gymnastics items were eliminated; and optional items were added in a category which gave consideration to local conditions (e.g., swimming in the south and ice skating in the north).[27]

The 1975 revised standards reflected both a re-evaluation of selected components of the earlier programme and a retention of those items felt to be appropriate. They established classification by age and sex as well as standards of performance in five or six activities. The four age-groups are for children (10–12 yrs.), juniors—I (13–15) and II (16–17) and young people (18 and older). Those in the children's and the I group have five compulsory activities and one optional activity (the latter determined by provinces, municipalities and autonomous regions), while the II and youth group have six compulsory and one optional. In all cases the compulsory activities are determined and set nationally.

In attempting to popularise the revised programme, China's sports leaders have realised that vigorous promotional effort is required, without which only limited results can accrue. The following "Regulations" were therefore issued with the new standards and serve to illustrate both the content and, in broad terms, the means of implementation of the programme.

1. The Regulations and Standards for the National Physical Training Programme (hereafter cited as the 'Programme') are drawn up in order to carry out the directives set by our Great Leader, Chairman Mao: "Promote physical culture, build up the people's health" and "Our educational policy should enable everyone who receives an education to develop morally, intellectually and physically and become a worker with both socialist consciousness and culture." They are to encourage children, young people and teenagers to take up physical training for the sake of the revolution and to promote normal physical growth, to build up their health, and to improve sports standards so as to serve proletarian politics, workers, peasants and soldiers and productive labour.

2. The Programme shall be practised extensively in the schools and the People's Liberation Army. Factories, mines, government offices and rural people's communes shall implement the standards according to local conditions.

3. The Programme has been designed for four groups: children aged 10–12 years; juniors (I) aged 13–15 years; juniors (II) aged 16–17 years; and youths aged 18 and over. Different standards have been set for males and females in each age group.

4. The Programme has been developed to promote all-round development in terms of suppleness, stamina, speed and strength. Athletics and gymnastics events form the basis of the programme. In the children's and junior (I) groups there are six events, five of which are compulsory. The junior (II) and youth groups have seven events, six of which are compulsory. In all four groups the optional event shall be selected by each province, municipality and autonomous region according to local conditions in a manner which contributes to the overall uniformity of the nationwide programme.

5. Insofar as the level of and facilities for physical culture and sport vary throughout the country, supplementary programmes shall be implemented as desirable in local units. Army units shall also consider the needs and directives of the General Staff and the General Political Department.

6. Those taking the Programme's physical fitness tests must, beginning with the passing of their first test, also pass all other items in their age group within one year (items passed more than a year before must be passed again). Lower age group participants may proceed to the next group upon successful completion of all tests. Guidance to scientific principles of training, safety and individual levels of fitness must be given. "Commandism" and formalism shall be avoided and tests shall be given only on the basis of regular training over a period of time. Training shall continue after completion of the tests so as to continue to develop the individual's health and improve his standard in sports.

7. Implementation of the Programme will require sports grounds, equipment and facilities, and coaching which shall be provided by relying on the masses and undertaken in a spirit of self reliance and hard work, diligence and thrift. Additional equipment shall be acquired as needed.

8. In order to carry out this work well, it is necessary conscientiously to study Chairman Mao's instructions on the theory of the dictatorship of the proletariat, to uphold the basic line of the Party, and to apply Mao's thought to physical culture and sport. It is necessary constantly to conduct educational work on Chairman Mao's revolutionary line in physical culture and sport, in preparation against war, in physical culture and health knowledge among the masses, in affirming the objectives and methods of training, in conducting revolutionary mass criticism and repudiation, and in eliminating the influence of the revisionist line on physical culture and sport and to raise the consciousness of the people in taking an active part in physical training for the sake of the revolution.

9. The Programme shall be implemented under the unified leadership of the Party. Physical culture and sports committees at various levels shall coordinate the programme under the leadership of local revolutionary committees. Education departments, the People's Liberation Army and trade unions shall provide leadership in the relevant units of their systems. Medical and health workers shall be responsible for the supervision of medical care. The Youth League, women's groups, Red Guards, Little Red Soldiers, and other mass organisations shall play an active part in implementing the regulations.

10. These regulations shall take effect throughout the country on the day of their promulgation. Units which have implemented the Programme with good results, and individuals who have passed the tests, shall be commended by the localities and units concerned. [28]

Accompanying the regulations was an article in the Chinese press entitled "Take Up Physical Training for the Sake of the Revolution" [29] which encouraged active support for the new programme. Tables 1 and 2* provide details of the standards for the youngest and oldest groups.

When observing the fitness programme of the Chinese for the first time, Westerners generally respond in one of two ways. Either they are concerned at what they consider to be regimented people following orders as to where, when and how to engage in exercise, or they return with the notion that all people in China have organised exercise. Neither view is totally correct. Exercise in China is not mandatory, it is rather encouraged. What one sees in one area of China will not necessarily be encountered elsewhere; each region varies. Nor is the entire exercise programme free of problems. The long-standing belief of older people and those in strenuous physical occupations that they do not need special exercise is still prevalent. What does exist in China today is a broad fitness programme designed for mass participation and depending for success on the interest shown by provincial and local officials.

Participation by the populace in recreation varies greatly according to the age, occupation and domicile of the individual, and of course the

* This Table 2 may be compared with a similar age-category table of standards for Soviet citizens: see Table 3 on pp. 40–1 [Ed.].

facilities available (this latter aspect will be covered below). In urban areas, recreational pursuits are enjoyed after the eight-hour workday and on the single day off each week allotted to all workers. Diversions such as hiking, strolling in the parks and zoos, boating, ice skating (in northern areas), visiting museums, viewing films, and attending cultural and sports events comprise activities engaged in publicly, while cards and table games are often pursued at home. Although most Westerners look upon cycling as a leisure pursuit, in China it is primarily a means of transport for most people. In addition to the above-mentioned pastimes, urban dwellers often take part in sport at neighbourhood or workers' cultural palaces.

For those residing in a country setting such as a commune, again

Table 1. CHILDREN'S GROUP

	Events/Items	10–12 years	
		Males	Females
1	60-Metre dash	10.3 sec.	10.8 sec.
2	400-Metre run	1:30.0 min.	1:40.0 min
	or Skipping (number of times in 90 seconds)	170	190
3	High jump	1.00 m.	0.95 m.
	or Long jump	3.00 m.	2.80 m.
4	Hand-grenade throw—(300g)	23.00 m.	18.00 m.
	or Baseball throw	30.00 m.	20.00 m.
	or Pole rope climb—(4 limbs)	2.80 m.	2.00 m.
5	Gymnastics	according to standards*	
6	Swimming—(25 metres)	any stroke, no time limit	
	or Skating or other event†		

* Items are in the miscellaneous skills category and consist of elementary tumbling moves

† Items in this category are determined by conditions in individual provinces, municipal districts and autonomous regions

Table 2.   YOUTH GROUP

Events/Items	Over 18 years	
	Males	Females
1 100-metre dash	14.0 sec	16.5 sec.
or 200-metre dash (men)	29.0 sec.	
2 800-metre run (women)		3:25.0 min.
1500-metre run (men)	5:45.0 min.	
or 3,000-metre run (men)	12:50.0 min.	
3 High jump	1.25 m.	1.10 m.
or Long jump	4.50 m.	3.40 m.
4 Chin-ups (men)	9	
Push-ups (women)	12	9
or Parallel bar dips (men)	12	
or Sit-ups (women)		10
or Pole/rope climb—(men: 2 hands)	3.50 m.	
—(women: 4 limbs)		3.10 m.
5 Hand-grenade throw—(men: 700g)	36.00 m.	
—(women: 500g)		23.00 m.
or Shot put—(men: 5k)	7.40 m.	
—(women: 4k)		6.00 m.
6 Gymnastics	according to standards*	
7 Military outing with back pack		
—(men: 5k weight for 10km. distance)	65 min.	
—(women: 3k weight for 6 km. distance)		45 min.
or Swimming—(men: 100 metres)	any stroke, no time limit	
—(women: 100 metres)		
or Skating or other event†		

   * Items are in four categories:
vaulting horse, parallel bars,
horizontal bar and miscellaneous
skills

   † Items in this category are
determined by conditions in
individual provinces, municipal
districts and autonomous regions

conditions vary. Obviously, parks, museums, and zoos are not readily available to these people; however, the other leisure pursuits mentioned are taken up when work is over. Cultural and sports performances take place and often amusements are organised by the commune.

In conclusion, exercise and recreational programme are generally available for most people throughout China, with each locale varying in the degree to which people participate. Urban residents have, as a rule, many more opportunities for participation in recreational activities, while the rural population possesses limited resources and time in which to enjoy such pursuits. Chinese involvement in leisure and recreation is likely to increase substantially in future as productivity increases and allows more time for such activities.

(ii) Sports, games and competitions

All segments of Chinese society have opportunities to participate in a broad range of sporting activities at various levels of competition. Besides physical education classes in schools, individuals have opportunities for playing a sport in the "spare-time sports schools", at workplaces, in the military or on the commune. For proficient athletes, national and international competition exists.

(a) Physical education in schools. The responsibility for physical education in China generally rests with local authorities. It is, therefore, difficult to generalise about a "typical" physical education programme. There are some basic elements though to which all such programmes adhere. To begin with, most pupils at urban primary (ages 6–11) and middle (11–16) schools participate in a required forty-five-minute P.E. class twice a week. In rural areas, classes vary according to conditions and facilities, but would not usually exceed this number. Some schools in China are presently experimenting with daily physical education, but this is the exception rather than the rule. Universities and technical colleges also require students to participate in regular physical education classes; but here, too, the exact number of times per week varies with each institution. For example, in recent years Peking University has required all students to attend physical education classes twice weekly for one hour on each occasion.

P.E. classes at primary and middle schools are, for the most part, coeducational, with appropriate sex differentiation according to the activities engaged in and, where needed, competition levels. Urban classes do not mix ability levels while rural schools are often forced to do so owing to the relatively small numbers of pupils. University P.E. classes likewise are normally coeducational and are usually conducted along departmental lines: for example, Chemistry students would attend class together. In most cases specific gym attire is not worn save for tennis shoes.

For handicapped children (blind, deaf, dumb), special schools exist and opportunities are similar to those found in regular schools. Thus, the students at the Guangzhou deaf-mute school in Canton participate in morning exercise programmes, regular P.E. classes and after-school sports.

Activities offered vary with each province and school since no national syllabus exists. Generally at the primary level, youngsters would be introduced to such activities as Chinese skipping, apparatus gymnastics, casual ball games, tug-of-war, tag games, relays and *wushu* along with morning exercise and military-related activities (hand-grenade throwing). Northern areas would include ice sports in the curriculum. At this level, emphasis is placed on the development of physical fitness and motor skills and the acquisition of positive attitudes towards lifetime participation in physical culture. To these ends, cooperative rather than competitive, elimination-type activities are emphasised. In an effort to encourage greater achievement at the initial learning stages, scaled-down equipment is often used.

Activities available to middle school children, in addition to those previously mentioned, provide for greater emphasis on team games and individual fitness activities, including volleyball, athletics, gymnastics, soccer, badminton and, the most popular of all, basketball. Equally popular, but found generally as a recreational activity in the school playground, is table tennis. Besides these activities, many middle schools now include the National Physical Training Programme as part of the curriculum to evaluate student fitness levels. In comparison to primary schools, middle schools tend to offer more elimination-type activities in their classes while still attempting to develop favourable attitudes toward active participation and physical fitness. University and technical college students take part in activities similar to the middle schools, but they have a less structured programme allowing more individual choice. At this level, emphasis is placed on lifetime participation and fitness for economic production. At all three levels of education, the activities offered entail readily-available, inexpensive equipment which allows large groups to participate (tug-of-war, relay races, tumbling, etc.). Classes tend to be large, sometimes as many as sixty students, thus making specific individualised instruction difficult. As a result, teaching methods are generally teacher-centred at the middle school and college levels. Very young children, however, receive loving care from kindergarten and nursery staff which seems to result in a confidence seldom seen in Western children.

(b) *Spare-time sports schools.* Opportunities exist at most schools and universities for students to participate in individual and team competitive sport, although these are greater in the towns than in the countryside. For those primary and middle school pupils who show sports potential, special coaching is provided at the spare-time sports schools. First begun in 1955, over 1,500 such schools exist today throughout China serving over 100,000 youngsters.[30] Pupils are selected for attendance at these schools on the basis of their school academic record, potential sporting ability, and recommendations from teachers and schoolmates. Each school differs in its training schedule, some schools offering pupils a weekly training session, others a daily after-school session, and still others a boarding arrangement where athletes complete their school-work in the morning and train in the afternoon.

One example of a spare-time sports school is Shihshahai in Peking. Here, over 900 pupils receive coaching from a staff of 150 in such activities as *wushu*, table tennis, basketball, volleyball, weightlifting, chess, gymnastics, ice skating and ice hockey.[31] Most pupils at these schools study and train in only one sport and many of them remain at the school for three or four years. While opportunities to attend such schools are naturally limited, school authorities have attempted to ensure that the knowledge gained by students is disseminated as widely as possible. Thus, spare-time school pupils often return to their schools and neighbourhoods and share their experience and newly-acquired skills with their classmates and peers.

(c) *Local competitions*. School pupils, factory and office workers, military personnel and rural commune members arrange, in cooperation with representatives of the All-China Sports Federation and other government agencies, sports competitions on a regular basis. There are few world sports, with the exception of boxing, which are not practiced today by the Chinese. But the range of sports is not restricted to the popular Western range of activities; it also includes ancient Chinese sports. This continuation of ancient sporting traditions was specifically encouraged by the Chinese government in 1953 when it sponsored a traditional sports contest at Tianjin which included displays of weight-lifting, traditional forms of wrestling, archery, horsemanship and martial arts (*taijiquan*, *wushu*).[32] The interest and involvement in these traditional events, revived two decades ago, continues to the present. Sports that require expensive equipment and facilities, while not entirely neglected, have yet to be promoted on a large scale: such activities as tennis, rowing, power boating and similar activities of an individual nature are slowly being expanded.

At local level, the organisation of sports competitions is the responsibility of the unit involved. Thus, factory sports committees arrange both intra- and inter-factory sports competitions. Within each of the four categories mentioned (schools, factories/offices, communes and the military) contests vary in emphasis and organisation according to interest, resources and leadership. Military competitions often stress such skills as parachuting, marksmanship and para-military activities. Communes tend to offer sports which require inexpensive equipment, such as basketball or volleyball.

Certain sections of the country are noted for their expertise in specific sports. For example, Taishan is considered the volleyball county of China while Dongkuan is the swimming county. One sporting activity universally engaged in is long-distance running, particularly during the "spring festival". Teams representing schools or work units compete in "round-the-city-races" or in mass distance running. In the urban areas, district and city-wide tournaments are held in most sports to determine local champions; local representatives can advance to provincial and national championships in some sports.

(d) *National competitions.* In recent years, two types of national competitions have been held in China. National championships are, as a rule, held annually in each sport (see Table 3 for dates of initial championships). National competitions also take place in the form of "National Games" not unlike those of the Soviet *Spartakiads*. These games have been held three times up to 1978 (1959, 1965 and 1975). In 1975, at the Third National Games, 10,000 junior and senior male and female competitors participated in a variety of events: the junior programme consisted of eight events, while the senior programme of twenty-three events included ball games, athletics, gymnastics, acro-

Table 3   FIRST NATIONAL CHAMPIONSHIPS IN SELECTED SPORTS

Year	Sports
(1947)*	Soccer
1951	Basketball, Volleyball
1952	Swimming, Table Tennis
1953	Boxing, Ice Sports, Tennis, Athletics, Gymnastics, Cycling, Traditional Sports (Display)
1955	Mountaineering
1956	Badminton, Rowing, Yachting
1957	Chess
1958	Marathon, Gliding, Parachuting
1974	Baseball

* Held in liberated areas of the country

Sources: *People's China, China Reconstructs, Peking Review, Tiyu Bao.*

batics, swimming, diving, water polo, weightlifting, shooting, archery, fencing, traditional martial arts (*wushu*), cycling, Chinese and international chess and *weiqi* (go). Teams were entered from each of China's provinces including, for the first time, Taiwan.[33] In addition to these Games, regular national competitions have been held by the People's Liberation Army: most recently the Third All-China Army Sports Competitions took place in Peking in 1975, involving 5,000 men and women in eighteen events ranging from rifle shooting, bayoneting and hand-grenade throwing to swimming, weightlifting and soccer. A special feature of recent national competitions has been the holding of the events in outlying areas using community facilities as well as in a single central stadium.

(*e*) *International competition.* Involvement in international competition by teams and individuals representing the People's Republic of China has been both extensive and irregular. In the decade following liberation, the Chinese competed extensively with both socialist and non-socialist nations. Political disagreements over the recognition and representation of Taiwan in international sporting organisations provoked China's withdrawal, in 1958, from several international sports governing bodies, including the International Olympic Committee. Notwithstanding these events, China continued to compete in numerous international competitions and played host to the 26th World Table Tennis Championships in 1961. China chose further to reduce contacts in the international arena from 1965 to 1969—the period of the Cultural Revolution.

China's notice of her intention to re-enter international competition took the form of an announcement, in November 1970, that a male high jumper, Ni Zhi-jin, had set a world record. Following this, Chinese athletes emerged to participate internationally in basketball and table tennis. Four years later, China took part in the Seventh Asian Games held in Teheran. Since then, China has increased her participation in international sport considerably. By 1976, the individual sports associations affiliated to ACSF were members of thirteen international sport federations (FIBA, FILA, FIVB, FHI, FIE, FISA, FIC, ISU, IIHF, ITTF, FISU, ISF, FIDE).

Numerous world records have been set by Chinese athletes, most notably in archery, pistol shooting and weightlifting. Both men and women competitors also continue to enjoy success at international table tennis tournaments. In spite of the growing Western awareness of Chinese sport and China's membership of several international federations, recognition of the People's Republic of China by the International Olympic Committee had, by early 1978, still not occurred.

A visit to Peking during 1977 by IOC President, Lord Killanin, has as yet not resulted in resolution of the question of recognition.

IV. *Training of sports personnel*

The Chinese system of training sports and physical education personnel is, in many respects, similar to that found in other socialist countries. The sharing of ideas and expertise among the socialist nations which characterised the 1950s saw China adopt many of the teaching methods, curricula, training methods and award systems of both the Soviet Union and the German Democratic Republic. The past decade has, however, witnessed the emergence of several unique approaches in China's continuing search for Chinese solutions to problems of Chinese education. These new directions are still experimental and are expected to continue in this vein for several years. What is evident is that education has changed markedly from what it was under its early Soviet influence.

(i) *Institutes of physical culture*

The preparation of physical culture and sports personnel is not a major responsibility of the universities in China, but is carried on in special training colleges and institutes. At the start of 1978, there were eight institutes of physical culture (Chengdu [Chengtu], Peking, Shanghai, Shenyang, Tianjin, Wuhan, Xian [Sian] and the People's Liberation Army Physical Culture Institute located in Guangzhou [Canton]). During the last quarter-century the number and location of institutes has fluctuated from two in 1952 (Chengdu and Shanghai) to six in 1953 and ten in 1958. This last figure remained constant until the Cultural Revolution (1966) at which time the institutes, like most of the nation's schools, colleges and universities, were closed. In the early 1970s the institutes once again began opening their doors, but have not yet reached the pre-1966 total.

The Peking Institute of Physical Culture, established 1 November 1953, is representative of physical culture institutes found throughout the country. Situated in the northwestern district of the city, the Institute's facilities include three gymnasiums, two table tennis halls, two volleyball-cum-basketball halls, one weightlifting hall, separate gymnastics and *wushu* buildings, an indoor track, an indoor 50-metre swimming pool with underwater observation windows, classrooms and administration halls and lecture rooms, along with sixty outdoor teaching stations including facilities for baseball, handball, basketball, volleyball, soccer, athletics, rifle shooting, motor cycling, swimming and ice skating.[34] Local conditions naturally influence the nature of each institute. For example, the Wuhan complex is located on the picturesque East Lake while the Xian Institute is situated in the city's southwestern light industrial district. Training opportunities also exist at spare-time sports schools, work units, teacher training colleges and other educational institutions. In addition, provincial training centres have been established in several areas of the country, often in conjunction with existing community facilities, schools and colleges, thereby taking advantage of available amenities.

(ii) Programmes and courses

At present the focus and direction of all Chinese education, physical culture included, are undergoing re-examination in the light of the experiments of the early 1970s. Several changes appear imminent, including increased emphasis on research and graduate studies and a return to examinations. These emerging trends should not be interpreted as a return to the old ways, but rather as an application of new methods in response to the present and future needs of the country for technological and scientific development in the 1980s.

The nature of the programmes available at the institutes varies since, as at primary and middle schools, there is no nationwide curriculum. Basic guidelines exist which are applied to local conditions and needs. Thus, a measure of uniformity is obtained without resorting to rigid dogma and stipulations which may have little applicability in certain areas, particularly in national minority regions. Following the Cultural Revolution, new experiments in education were based, to a large measure, on a directive adopted on 8 August 1966:

The teaching material should be thoroughly transformed, in some cases beginning with simplifying complicated material. While their main task is to study, students should also learn other things. That is to say, in addition to their studies they should also learn industrial work, farming and military affairs, and take part in the struggles of the cultural revolution to criticise the bourgeoisie as these struggles occur.[35]

Applied to physical culture and sport, this policy resulted in several experimental approaches being undertaken during the first half of the 1970s.

In the selection of students, the policy has been to require applicants to have at least two or three years of practical experience, to be at least twenty years old, physically fit for work, unmarried, and to have completed middle school. In addition, recommendations have been required from both teachers and school- or workmates, with the final decision on acceptance resting with the institute concerned. While there have been exceptions (e.g., students demonstrating an aptitude for foreign languages), educational opportunities beyond middle school would seem to be regarded as a privilege and not a right, the benefits of which would be applied in "serving the people". Recent announcements suggest that more flexibility will be applied in the future, including a return to some form of entrance examination and the possible reduction in the importance attached to recommendations from school- and workmates. Unlike the changes in the selection process, the experimental teaching methodology has for the most part proven advantageous and is expected to continue.

Teaching techniques and methods used in training physical culture personnel have likewise undergone change. No longer is the lecture the main teaching method; rather the concept of "open door schooling" is to be found in all institutions. Lectures are now integrated with practical work experience in the community. Experienced physical culture workers visit classes and students conduct "social investigations" in neighbourhoods, factories, communes and offices. The purpose of these varied experiences is to combine teaching, scientific research and production in meeting the needs of the student and of society. For example, in order to have physical culture serve the workers, peasants and soldiers as well as to provide opportunities for students to learn from these groups, a number of students and teachers from the Peking Institute have visited the Capital Iron and Steel Company, a colliery and a local bus terminal to investigate work habits and the effectiveness of specific exercise programmes for the workers. At the bus terminal, data was collected on forty-five drivers including on weight, grip strength, reaction time, pulse rates, movements made while driving, and general working conditions. As a result, a new exercise programme was designed and implemented to meet the specific demands of the job situation. Procedures such as these reflect Mao's directive that "those who would be teachers of the people must first be students of the people". There is little to indicate that policies such as these will be altered radically in the near future.

Teaching materials have also undergone changes in recent years which further reflect the integration of theory and practice. Some courses have been shortened and certain redundant aspects, such as the frequently overlapping areas of health, anatomy and physiology, have been combined or altered more easily to fit a sequential teaching order. When most institutes reopened in 1970-1, courses required two years for completion. By 1975, the time had been extended to three years and plans were being made for the resumption of post graduate studies in physical culture. It would seem that four- and five-year courses to meet the demands of the population generally and of competitive athletes will appear in the not-so-distant future. Finally, short courses, community-based clinics, and mobile units serving remote regions complement opportunities for the training and study of physical culture and sport. In addition to all these programmes are the extensive services of the People's Sports Publishing House and the local physical culture committees which provide printed material for all regions of the country, often in the local as well as Han dialects.

Although no national figures are available regarding the number of students who have completed training courses, between 1953 and 1975 more than 8,400 graduated from the Peking Institute.[36] By comparison, only 440 students graduated from the normal school which operated for thirty years prior to liberation. Chinese officials admit that the number of trained individuals is far from adequate and thus, as a temporary measure, short courses have been offered in an attempt to train additional coaches, teachers and officials.

In the area of curriculum, all eight physical culture institutes adhered to the following basic pattern during the early and mid-1970s:

1. Political Science: Marxism–Leninism–Mao Zedong Thought.
2. Work and Productive Labour: practical experience (on the commune, in the factory and in the militia for a certain period of each study year).
3. Theory of Physical Culture: administration, health, and community and group organisation skills.
4. Activities: swimming, table tennis, *wushu*, athletics, gymnastics and team sports.
5. Optional courses and areas of specialisation.[37]

In recent years, the formal curricula and training courses for coaches in specific sports have been supplemented by exchange visits and attendance at international conferences. Chinese ice hockey coaches have attended seminars, clinics and training camps in Canada and soccer coaches have done likewise in the German Democratic Republic. In March 1977, the Chinese Badminton Association hosted a clinic in Peking for foreign coaches and officials and indications are that Chinese participation both at home and abroad will increase in the coming years.

The state accepts the responsibility for placement of students upon completion of their courses, students often returning to the production units from which they came. With the present emphasis on improving conditions and opportunities in rural areas, many students, including those receiving training in physical culture, are sent to work in the countryside to work with and learn from commune members. Graduates have a limited choice to select, in consultation with state and local officials, their placements from approved postings in schools, commercial units, factories and government offices, in addition to those listed in rural areas; they continue to be involved in productive labour, group study programmes and other institutions of society while providing their services to members to the unit or neighbourhood concerned.

V. *Facilities and equipment*

With a present population in excess of 800 million, both the popularisation of mass sport and the raising of national and international standards have been limited by the availability of and access to facilities and equipment. What is noteworthy, however, is not that China has yet to satisfy fully the demands of her vast population for stadiums, gymnasiums, swimming pools, playing fields, ice hockey skates, volleyballs, rowing shells or track suits, but rather that the country has progressed as far as it has in barely three decades. At the end of World War II, many of the nation's facilities lay in ruin and disrepair. Those which had escaped the ravages of war were located in large urban areas, inaccessible to a large majority of the population. In addition, the production of sports equipment was severely curtailed during the war years, resulting in the need to import many of the items required.

A recent survey of selected major facilities showed the following comparison with those available at the time of liberation.

Table 4.   SELECTED MAJOR COMMUNITY FACILITIES IN CHINA

Facility	1949	1975
Stadiums	16	151
Gymnasiums	13	113
Swimming Pools	92	1,602

Source: *China Reconstructs. No. 12, December 1975.*

Not included in these figures are the thousands of neighbourhood playing fields, factory courts, commune sports halls, and natural waterways used for both recreation and competition. On the one hand, Chinese technology and scientific skill have been tapped at provincial and national level to provide facilities which meet exacting international standards. On the other, the millions of peasants have not "gone without" despite the state's decision to centralise its major resources in the urban areas of Shanghai and Peking. Following the principles of "self-reliance", most schools, factories, offices and communes assess their specific needs, design appropriate facilities and undertake the necessary construction, in consultation with physical culture personnel, but without taxing the state's central resources. Everywhere one travels in China one finds playing fields, games rooms, swimming pools and recreation halls designed and built by the local residents. The quality and nature of the facilities of course vary throughout the country, but few if any regions fail to provide at least some physical space for sport and recreation. New stadiums and sports grounds have recently been built in various parts of the country, including in the Tibetan capital Lhasa;[38] all provincial capitals have become sites for small but comprehensive sports complexes.

China's major sporting complex is in Peking and is similar to Moscow's Luzhniki Park. The Workers' Stadium, built in 1958 on reclaimed marshland, seats 80,000 spectators mainly to watch athletics and soccer; the stadium also contains accommodation for 1,500 athletes, shops, stores, dining facilities, medical treatment rooms and training areas housed under one roof. Adjacent to the stadium are indoor and outdoor pools, a diving tank and a man-made lake for aquatic and ice sports. To the west of the stadium lies the Workers' Gymnasium. Seating 15,000, the building's well-designed exit system enables the complex to be emptied in five to seven minutes. The Capital Gymnasium, located near the university district, was built during the Cultural Revolution and is the site of major table tennis, basketball and gymnastics competitions as well as cultural performances, conferences and receptions. Noted for its retractable floor which exposes a full-size ice hockey surface, the building was, until recently, the only artificial ice hockey rink in the country. A recent addition in Peking is a new baseball stadium situated in the southern district of Fengtai, while China's newest major sports structure is located in the nation's largest city, Shanghai. The Shanghai building's 110-metre suspended-ceiling construction provides unrestricted viewing from each of the 18,000 seats.[39] Photo-electric timing and scoring devices, electrically-controlled moveable stands, and basketball backboards and volleyball standards which automatically retract into the gymnasium floor make Shanghai's Indoor Stadium one of the world's most modern and technologically-advanced facilities. Without a doubt, Chinese technology has progressed to a stage where the nation can host the Olympic Games with ease should the political circumstances surrounding her membership be resolved.

In addition to these and other major urban complexes, smaller facilities, including cycling tracks, shooting ranges, tennis courts and multi-purpose halls, are being built throughout China. Physical culture personnel are well aware, however, that the provision of facilities is far from being equitable, with opportunities in the rural areas lagging behind the major populated centres. In an attempt to overcome these inequalities, regions as well as individual production units continue to emphasise local initiative and self-reliance. Of the many examples cited by Chinese officials, the accomplishments of the Lingchuan Machinery Factory in Sichuan (Szechuan) province are typical of those in most areas of the country: workers at the factory drained and cleaned old ditches to build a swimming pool, erected basketball courts and provided seating on an adjacent hillside, and constructed ping-pong tables and gymnastics apparatus for use by factory members.[40] The value of such policies which encourage decentralisation of facilities and local self-sufficiency was never more in evidence than at the Third National Games when, of the 197 venues used, 165 were attached to factories, communes and schools and were not public community facilities. Not only did these local sites provide the facilities required, but the scheduling of competitions in several locations made it possible for a larger and more diverse group of spectators at attend, thus further promoting sport among those members of the community who might not otherwise have observed the Games' events.

Factories which manufacture sports equipment are to be found in most large cities. There is virtually no item of equipment which is not produced in China—from shoes, basketballs and swim suits to stop watches, racing bicycles, tennis rackets and, of course, table tennis balls. In addition to specific sporting goods manufacturing enterprises, other factories contribute their expertise to meet the particular demands of certain sports. For example, a garment factory in Shanghai designed and produced the down and woollen clothing and the light-weight tents used in the successful ascent of Qomolungma Feng (Mount Everest) in 1975.[41] When officials required new scientific timing devices for use at the Third National Games, they likewise turned to the experts and ultimately selected models developed by workers at the Yunnan Electrical Equipment Factory in Kunming.[42]

Although China has the technological expertise to produce modern, durable equipment for use by her millions of athletes, foreigners travelling in the country have often observed that worn, second-rate equipment is used and go on to conclude that the Chinese are unable to produce quality shoes, balls and other sporting goods items. Such conclusions fail to recognise two major policy decisions which have emerged in recent years. First, China exports much of her high-quality sports equipment as the return in foreign capital is then made available for overall economic development. Second, one of China's major international commitments has been to the developing countries of the Third World and one of the many forms of friendly contact with these nations has been through sport: thus much of China's equipment is made available to the countries of Asia, Africa and Latin America. China has also contributed technical expertise and manpower to assist several Third World countries in the construction of major facilities, including a 30,000 seat stadium completed in 1977 in Somalia.[43] These policy decisions, not Chinese inability to produce equipment and build amenities, are the major reasons behind appeals to the population to be resourceful and self-reliant. As in the case of the provision of facilities, officials are aware of the shortcomings and, as part of current economic planning designed to raise the material well-being of all citizens, programmes are being drawn up to increase the production and availability of all forms of equipment.

VI. *Concluding comments*

Since the establishment of the People's Republic in 1949, sport and physical culture have received continuing attention from Party, state and mass organisations at all levels. In comparison to the conditions which existed during the first half of the twentieth century, the results and accomplishments of the past three decades are undeniable. Health and fitness are mutually integrated and universally promoted. Equipment and facilities of varying types are provided throughout China's many regions. Games and competitions are held at local, national and international levels with increasing frequency. Full-time and part-time courses are being conducted to satisfy the needs for teachers, coaches and officials. In a word, physical culture has become an integral part of contemporary Chinese society.

People's China remains, however, a developing country. Notwithstanding the accomplishments, ranging from the provision of universal basic medical care and primary education to the development of a nuclear capability and a space satellite programme, much remains to be done. Several shortcomings in China's current development of physical culture have been noted: regular participation on a mass basis is still far from satisfactory; the availability of and access to equipment and facilities are not yet equitable; training courses have yet to produce the number of personnel required throughout the country; and, until recently, international contacts have been limited to a degree which has proved detrimental to the development of mutual understanding and the sharing of technical expertise. The Chinese, it should be noted, deny none of these shortcomings. Furthermore, it is reasonable to assume that, as material conditions improve—resulting, for example, in more leisure time—new problems will emerge and new challenges appear.

Following the principles of "weeding through the old to bring forth the new" and "making the past serve the present and foreign methods serve China", the traditions of four millenia have been and continue to be integrated into the realities of the twentieth century. One key to China's success is the application of the experience of others to the solution of Chinese problems by the Chinese, in a Chinese way. On the one hand, the approach has been to encourage flexibility, such as through the integration of theory and practice and the implied ac-

ceptance of the "change" which results. Thus, much of what is occur-
ring in education is experimental and, while "trends" are identifiable,
definitive analysis remains tenuous. On the other hand, on questions of
principle, such as China's demand to be recognised as the sole legitimate
representative of Chinese athletes in international sport, there have
been and will continue to be no compromises.

Finally, in a world prone to pessimistic prognostications about the
future, Chinese optimism is refreshing. Acknowledging the urgent
need to accelerate the drive for modernisation and so to improve the
well-being of all Chinese citizens, the lines of a poem written in 1963
have relevance for the future:

So many deeds cry out to be done,
And always urgently;
The world rolls on,
Time presses.
Ten thousand years are too long,
Seize the day, seize the hour![44]

The Chinese way is unique. The People's Republic has forged a
separate path from the other socialist nations and has taken a road
designed to build China into a modern, prosperous nation. In a society
striving to "serve the people", physical culture has a clearly recognisable
rôle.

NOTES

1. Shi Ji-wen, Sports Go Forward in China, Peking, 1963, p. 3.

2. See Wu Wen-zhong, Zhongguo Tiyu Shi Tu Yanxi, Taibei, 1970, plates
pp. 13–20.

3. Shi, p. 2.

4. Wu, plates pp. 21–4.

5. Ibid.

6. Shi, p. 3.

7. See Donn F. Draeger and Robert W. Smith, Asian Fighting Arts, New
York, 1969.

8. See "An Ancient Form of Physical Culture", China Reconstructs, No. 8,
August 1955, p. 27.

9. Tiyu Bao, 30 May 1977.

10. See Jonathan Kolatch, Sport, Politics and Ideology in China, New York,
1972, pp. 8–11.

11. Zhu Ming-yi, "Physical Culture", in The Chinese Yearbook 1935–36,
Shanghai, 1936, pp. 541–53.

12. Chester Holcombe, The Real Chinaman, New York, 1895, p. 93.

13. Constitution of the People's Republic of China, Peking, 1975, Article 12.

14. The Common Programme and Other Documents of the First Plenary Session of
the Chinese People's Political Consultative Conference, Peking, 1950, Article 48.

15. *Documents of the First Plenary Session of the First National People's Congress of the People's Republic of China*, Peking 1955, Article 94.

16. Mao Zedong, "Tiyu Zhi Yanjiu", in Stuart R. Schram, *Une Etude de L'Education Physique*, Paris, 1962.

17. Mao Zedong, "Talk at the Reception for the Presidium of the Second National Congress of the Youth League (30 June, 1953)," in *Quotations from Chairman Mao Tse-tung*, Peking, 1967, p. 293.

18. Mao Zedong, *On the Correct Handling of Contradictions Among the People*, Peking, 1957.

19. Cited in "Sports in New China", *China Reconstructs* No. 12, December 1975, p. 3.

20. *Renmin Ribao*, 16 July 1976.

21. Personal interview, 5 October 1976.

22. He Long (Ho Lung), in addition to serving as Minister, held positions as Vice-Premier of the State Council, Vice-Chairman of the National Defence Council, Member of the Party Central Committee and Politburo, and was active in several military organisations. Recent changes following the overthrow of the "Gang of Four" have resulted in Wang Meng being reappointed to replace Zhuang (Chuang Tse-tung) who rose to prominence following more than a decade as the world's premier table tennis player. Prior to his appointment as Minister by the Fourth National People's Congress, Zhuang served as a leading member of the Chinese Table Tennis Association and the All-China Sports Federation.

23. *Renmin Ribao*, 21 August 1977.

24. "Everybody Does Exercises", *China Reconstructs*, No. 3, March 1972, p. 18.

25. Ibid.

26. "Exercises to Fit the Job", *China Reconstructs*, No. 11, November 1974, p. 30.

27. *Xinhua*, 26 October 1958.

28. "Guojia Tiyu Duanlian Biaozhun Tiaoli", *Xin Tiyu*, No. 5, May 1975, p. 10.

29. *Guangming Ribao*, 6 May 1975.

30. "Sports in New China", *China Reconstructs*, No. 12, December 1975, p. 3.

31. Information from personal visits in 1972 and 1975.

32. "The Traditional Sports of China", *People's China*, 1 January 1954, pp. 17–23.

33. "The Third National Games", *China Reconstructs*, No. 12, December 1975, pp. 30–35.

34. Information based on personal visits in 1972, 1974 and 1975.

35. *Decision of the Central Committee of the Chinese Communist Party Concerning the Great Proletarian Cultural Revolution*, Peking, 1966, p. 10.

36. Personal communication from staff of the Peking Institute of Physical Culture, June 1975.

37. Information based on discussions with teaching staff in China between 1972 and 1976.

38. "Sports on the Tibetan Plateau", *China Features*, January 1977.

39. "Sports Facilities in China", *China Reconstructs*, No. 12, December 1975, p. 37.

40. Ibid. See also "Athletic Equipment and Sports Gear Production in China", *China Features* (n.d. circa 1976).

41. *Da Gong Bao*, No. 472, 19 June 1975.

42. *Da Gong Bao*, No. 483, 4 September 1975.

43. *Da Gong Bao*, No. 597, 24 November 1977.

44. "Reply to Comrade Kuo Mojo" in *Mao Tse-tung Poems*, Peking, 1976, p. 46.

R. J. Pickering

CUBA

PERSONAL NOTE

Ron Pickering initially trained as a teacher at the College of St. Mark and St. John, Chelsea, London, before studying at the Carnegie College of Physical Education, Leeds. After a period of teaching and coaching he became National Athletics Coach to Wales and South West England, being responsible for the coaching of several international athletes, including the 1964 Olympic long-jump champion Lynn Davies. In 1967 he relinquished his post with the Amateur Athletic Association to become Recreational Manager of the Lee Valley Regional Park Authority, the first regional park to be developed in Britain. Between 1970 and 1973 he completed his M.Ed. at Leicester University, writing a thesis on "Factors Affecting the Performance of Young Athletes". Well known as sportswriter, athletics adviser and commentator, he has done much to popularise sport among young people through such TV programmes as "Superstars", "Sportstown" and "We are the Champions". He has written and edited a number of sports books, including British Athletics Yearbook (1974 onwards), Olympic Handbook (1976), Strength Training for Athletics (1965) and Shot Putting (1967). Married to former Olympic long-jump champion Jean Desforges, he has two children, Kim and Shaun.

CONTENTS

Preamble

Although there is still no universally acceptable definition of "comparative physical education and sport" it is clear that during the past decade or so the subject has attracted a good deal of attention from some able minds. Authors like D. W. J. Anthony[1] and M. L. Howell[2] have formulated the basic criteria for a comparative analysis of the dominant characteristics and developments within sport and physical education. Determined as I was to use their basic format as a guideline, I am now very conscious of the fact that I have had to adopt a much more empirical approach. Lack of time and even a basic knowledge of the Spanish language proved to be serious limitations, as was the comparative dearth of background reading matter. However, I was extremely fortunate to be given the opportunity to travel to Cuba on three separate occasions and the help that I and my colleagues from the BBC received was very considerable.

A word of explanation regarding my visits to Cuba may be of some interest to the reader. Having personally followed with great interest the progress of its athletes in particular at recent Olympic and Pan American Games, I managed to persuade the editor of the *Radio Times* that a visit might be warranted to obtain preview material prior to the Montreal Games of 1976. My first fact-finding tour was in March 1976 and there was so much of interest that I was determined to return —hopefully with a film unit to make a documentary television programme. The outstanding success of the Cuban team in Montreal promoted a good deal of attention from the media generally and the BBC then needed little prompting to give me the opportunity to visit Cuba again with a view to producing a documentary film on "Sport in Cuba". This was researched and filmed during November and December 1976 on behalf of the BBC television "World About Us" series for a programme due to be screened in the summer of 1977.

The world-wide reputation of the BBC meant that few doors were left unopened. We were able to view and film many and various schools, colleges, centres of excellence, training sessions, institutions, play centres, parks, etc., which provided a great deal of background for this documentary. Clearly my thanks are due to the BBC who made it

143

possible to develop the ideas put forward, especially Richard Taylor (the Producer) who more than shared my enthusiam for the project. However, he would be the first to agree with me that nothing would have been possible without the generous co-operation of the Cubans themselves. I would merely list the following as representing a vast group of friends and colleagues too numerous to mention:

Jorge Garcia Bango—General Director INDER (Instituto National de Deportes Educacion Fisica y Recreation);

Fabio Ruiz—Deputy Director, INDER;

Mario Rodriguez Escalona—Sub Director, Relaciones Internacionales, INDER;

Dr. Arnoldo Pallares—Director, Instituto de Medicina Deportiva;

Hiram Gonzales Alonzo—Director, Escuola Superior de Educacion Fisica;

Alberto Juantorena—athlete extraordinary.

I. *Historical, geographical and socio-political background*[3]

Territorially the Republic of Cuba is an archipelago of two main islands, Cuba and the Isle of Pines, together with numerous smaller islands, islets and cays—a combined area of 42,827 square miles (110,922 square kilometres). It lies in the Caribbean less than 100 miles south of Florida, USA, and within 200 miles of Jamaica, Haiti, the Bahamas and Mexico. The main island of Cuba is 745 miles long and its width varies between a mere 22 miles to 124 miles at its widest. Its climate is tropical with an average annual temperature of 77°F (25°C) and a rainy season from May to October during which hurricanes are frequent. Annual rainfall averages fifty-four inches.

According to the 1970 census, the total population of Cuba was just over 8·5 million, with 1·75 million living in Havana (La Habana) the capital. The Isle of Pines, now called the Isle of Youth, is the second largest island and has a permanent population of approximately 30,000. There are approximately one million Cuban exiles living in the United States, mainly Florida.

(i) *Ethnic origins and national composition*

For more than four centuries a wide variety of ethnic groups have been settling in Cuba, the predominant ones being Spanish and African. Others include Chinese, Europeans, Jews and Yucatecans, and contemporary Cuban society exhibits a remarkable ethnic diversity. Some of the earliest settlers came from the nearby islands of the Antilles, Bahamas and Haiti, and these constituted 80 per cent of the population at the time of the Spanish Conquest. From an estimated population of nearly 90,000, barely 5,000 survived the first 50 years of Spanish rule. Today there are only a few families living in the Orientel Mountains who display physical characteristics of the indigenous people.

More than 800,000 African slaves were imported by the Spaniards to work largely on the sugar plantations to replace the disappearing natives. These came from a wide variety of tribal backgrounds, but the most significant influx of any particular ethnic group was as recent as the early 1920s. More than 250,000 labourers were imported on contract from nearby Jamaica, Haiti and the other Antillean islands; and most of them remained.

Despite heavy white immigration to Cuba between the two world wars following a dramatic increase in the black birth rate, it is now estimated that about 45 per cent of the present population is either *mestizo* (mixed) or black. Now, with the breaking down of discrimination barriers, mixed marriages are increasing as Cuba moves towards an integrated society. All the same, it is important to stress that the black cultural influence has been considerable, especially in music, dance and sport.

Spanish is the Cuban national language with English taught as the second language and Russian third.

(ii) *Recent history*

In 1959, the dictatorship of General Fulgencio Batista was overthrown after years of guerrilla war led by Dr. Fidel Castro. Earlier, on 26 July 1953, Castro had led a suicidal attack on the military barracks of Moncada in Santiago and had been imprisoned on the Isle of Pines for two years before being granted amnesty. Castro then went to Mexico to prepare for another invasion and was joined by the Argentinian revolutionary "Che" Guevara.

The next invasion in 1956 was an almost total disaster, with a few survivors retreating to the Sierra Maestra Mountains to continue guerrilla warfare from there. As support in the countryside grew, they finally achieved victory and control in January 1959.

Although early political plans were vague, untested and largely idealistic, Castro's personal leadership brought him immense popularity. There followed the nationalisation of US-owned property worth hundreds of millions of dollars, which brought the undisguised hostility of the American Government; when in 1961 a group of Cuban exiles attempted to invade the island it was clear that they were heavily supported by the US administration.

Following this "Bay of Pigs" (Playa Giron) disaster the Americans cut off trading links with Cuba, which brought near economic disaster on the island. Not only had it lost its major importer of sugar, the US now imposed a complete blockade of Cuba. Castro's drift into Marxist–Leninist Communism was accelerated almost overnight, and the Soviet Union exchanged full diplomatic relations with Cuba in 1960, soon becoming its major trading partner with full military support.

In the early 1960s many Cubans, especially the wealthy and skilled, left the island for the United States; this weakened the administration but perhaps strengthened the resolve. The installation of Soviet missiles in 1962 almost precipitated a major war with the United States and the blockade with its resulting economic sanctions led to the rationing of food and clothing. With the substantial drop in the world price of sugar over recent years, Cuba's dependence on the Soviet Union has grown proportionately and its economic problems have become even more serious. Present-day (1978) rationing now includes sugar and cigars—two products for which Cuba is recognised as one of the world's major suppliers.

Recently several Latin American countries have re-established diplomatic relations with Cuba and during 1973 Cuba announced its wish to establish relations with the United States. Indeed, it pointed out that Cuba had never broken off relations in the first place, rather it had been at the American initiative. It would seem that relations between the two countries are now improving and the blockade is likely to be less of an obstacle in the future. Indeed, the "basketball initiatives" by US Senators McGovern and Abourezk in April 1977 succeeded in enabling the largest group of Americans to visit Cuba since 1961.[4]

In terms of sport, the previously enforced blockade meant limited competition, and a complete lack of sophisticated sports equipment or sporting exchanges with neighbouring countries. In effect, this meant exclusion from almost all the area and regional championships, which particularly affected sports like the Cuban national game of baseball confined as it is mainly to the Americas and Japan. The Soviet Union in particular, the Eastern Bloc generally, were quick to establish their own sports aid with coaches and advisers sent to set up training and teaching programmes. But quite apart from merely accepting the well-established Communist attitudes and priorities towards sport, Castro himself, a former National Squad basketball player, constantly stressed the importance of sport in terms of health, national fitness and especially national identity.

We want all children, all young people, the whole nation to practise sport. Above all sport is recreation, a healthy activity, a cultural activity for the people. That is why we are building schools all over the country to train physical education teachers. We shall have thousands of sports teachers and instructors; we shall have enough to send some to other Latin American countries. The day will come when they will want our instructors too. We are already receiving requests for instructors in boxing, basketball and pelota.[5]

Castro's personal charisma is very closely linked to his own identity with sportsmen and women. His speeches are reminiscent of a sporting Churchill during wartime, tinged with the *machismo* overtones of an Ernest Hemingway—a writer who is still venerated in Cuba.

The most important turning point in Cuba's international sporting history was its taking part in the 1966 Central American Games in Puerto Rica. Despite the blockade, it was determined to take part in the Games, even though Puerto Rica had decided not to provide visas or guarantee safe participation for Cubans. Rather than fly to Puerto Rica and be denied landing permission, the Cubans sent a ship with a full complement of athletes and officials. The story of the voyage of the *Cerro Pelado*, its hostile reception in San Juan, the harassment of the team, but Cuba's eventual total success in terms of dominating the medal tables, is now legend in Cuba. International sporting recognition began with that incident a little over a decade ago.

The Cubans admit that their revolution is far from complete and that they have had many failures on the way, but in terms of national pride, a real social awareness, educational reform and sporting achievement, they have made enviable progress. Much of that sporting progress has been made along similar lines to the other countries being discussed in this book: sport is believed to have enormous social and political significance and therefore, in common with the rest of the socialist world, is organised and run by a government department.

It has been suggested that one Teofilo Stevenson or Alberto Juantorena is worth one "Bay of Pigs" in international significance. Who can deny the impact that these and other Cuban athletes have made in the last decade or so? This course of events has led to much speculation and fascination throughout the world. To the Cubans who have been involved in the bitter struggle for recognition, it seems natural that they should now capitalise on their success in sporting and political terms. Thus, when in 1976, at the Olympic qualifying tournament for volleyball in Los Angeles, Cuba was drawn in the same regional qualification pool as the United States, yet did not lose a single set in the whole tournament, Fidel Castro described this as a "Sporting, psychological, patriotic and revolutionary victory".[6]

However, this chapter does not attempt simply to make an East–West comparison of political or even sporting ideologies. Each system, as Don Anthony suggests in his introduction, has its merits and demerits. It is simply an opportunity to pass on privileged information to those who share the view that Cuba has a very exciting story to tell regarding sport and physical education; of course, the Cubans themselves would be the first to admit they are still only a short way along their recently chosen path.

II. *Key factors to consider*

1. That out of the natural chaos of revolution it is only in the past decade or so that a pattern of sports development has really emerged, especially at international level;

2. that this is a country in which the dominant culture has been a Western one, onto which has been grafted a Marxist philosophy towards sport, with all that that means in terms of systemised training, government backing, financial support, enhanced national identity and pride based on results;

3. that this same country has an equable climate all the year round and an accepted tradition for producing natural athletes, as in rest of the Caribbean;

4. that Cuba is the first country in Central America and the Caribbean to ban professional sport.

It sounds rather like a professional coach's dream, but clearly these are just some of the contributory factors which might be worth examining when trying to evaluate the considerable and rapid sporting achievements of a country with a population less than that of London, New York or Tokyo.

III. *Pre-Revolutionary history and tradition of sport*

Cuba was one of the first countries to enter the Olympic record books, for it was one of twenty countries which took part in the Paris Games of 1900. Ramon Fonst became Cuba's first ever gold medallist by winning the épée event in fencing. He followed this in 1904 with two further gold medals, thus becoming the first man in Olympic history to win three individual gold medals. Indeed, the Cubans dominated the fencing events in 1900 and 1904, winning a total of twelve medals, including six golds. Fonst collected a fourth gold medal in the fencing team event by beating the only other team entered —a composite one consisting of two Americans and one Cuban!

Another, less serious, claim to fame came in the marathon at St. Louis. Felix Carragal, a Cuban postman, hitch-hiked to St. Louis and entered the marathon despite never having previously run in that or any other athletic event! An American athlete lent him his running gear and, despite stopping several times during the race to talk to bystanders, he still finished fourth and was dubbed "the Clown Prince of the Olympic Games".

Cuba gained no other Olympic medal successes prior to 1959; but perhaps its most talented athlete was Rafael Fortun, sprint champion of the Central American Games and Pan American Games who came to London for the 1948 Olympics and ran 10·3 sec. in his heat (the same time as the eventual winner) but whose lack of systemised training meant that in his progress through the heats he clocked slower times.

Cuba was one of the three founder members of the inaugural Central American and Caribbean Games in Mexico City in 1926; four years later it staged these Games in Havana with eleven countries taking part, It was at these Games that women participated for the first time, but were confined only to tennis. There is little doubt, however, that the vast majority of those who took part in such organised amateur sport were from the privileged classes who alone had access to private sports clubs. For the less privileged there was baseball—Cuba's national sport—in which one of the great attractions was the lure of a professional contract with an American major league club. Even today, more than fifteen years after the cessation of all professional sport in Cuba, there are still eight to ten top Cuban baseball players in the major American Leagues. For much the same reason, professional boxing also attracted a number of ordinary working people into its ranks.

One of the great attractions of Cuba as a tourist resort was the excellent opportunities for deep-sea fishing. Ernest Hemingway's "Old Man and the Sea" epitomised the challenge of the sport and enhanced the reputation of the Caribbean for it.

Clearly sport in pre-1959 Cuba was related to the class structure in terms of opportunities and facilities, and when the Revolution came there was ample political ammunition for changing the philosophy to "Sport for All". In Cuba today the slogans declare that sport is "the right of the people" and indeed mass participation is encouraged at every level. At the same time, like the rest of the socialist world, there is a considerable emphasis on "élitism", but now the opportunities are for those who show ability rather than for those who are privileged by wealth and can afford them. Two quotations from Castro make the point succinctly enough:

Of course, as the rich are not great athletes Cuba always looked ridiculous in any international competition. At the Olympics it was shameful to see the position occupied by Cuba because the rich, accustomed to good living, had not the necessary spirit of sacrifice to be good athletes. Good athletes must come from the people, from the working classes, from the lower strata, because they are capable of sacrifice; they can be consistent, tenacious; they can possess all the enthusiasm and interest needed to enter a competition and win.[7]

Imperialism has tried to humiliate Latin American countries, has tried to instil a feeling of inferiority in them. Let us say that it is part of the imperialists' ideology to present themselves as superior, and to develop in other peoples an inferiority complex. Sport has been used to that effect.[8]

IV. *International sport and post-Revolutionary Cuba*

With the exception of a tiny handful of outstanding Cuban athletes who had
occasionally won medals, Cuba had hardly ever won any medals in competition.
Yet nowadays we win medals in Central American, Pan American and even
Olympic competitions. . . . I can assure you that one of the things most admired
by our Latin American neighbours is our sporting successes. We can say that
our athletes are the children of our Revolution and, at the same time, the
standard-bearers of that same Revolution.[9]

Whilst it is convenient to consider Cuba's recent international
sporting successes, it is only fair to point out that what are now regarded
as major regional championships had fairly humble origins. The first

Table 1.   MEDALS OBTAINED BY CUBA SINCE 1959 IN
MAJOR CHAMPIONSHIPS

	Year	Medal Total	Gold	Silver	Bronze	Position in unofficial points table
Central American Games:						
Jamaica	1962	52	12	20	20	3rd
Puerto Rica	1966	190	96	33	61	1st
Panama	1970	363	207	95	61	1st
Santo Domingo	1974	321	225	57	39	1st
Pan American Games:						
Chicago	1959	20	2	11	7	11th
Sao Paulo	1963	44	21	9	14	6th
Winnipeg	1967	127	11	48	68	3rd
Cali	1971	254	82	101	71	2nd
Mexico	1975	275	119	94	62	2nd
Olympic Games:						
Rome	1960	0	0	0	0	45th
Tokyo	1964	1	0	1	0	42nd
Mexico	1968	10	0	10	0	23rd
Munich	1972	22	3	1	18	13th
Montreal	1976	13	6	4	3	8th

Source: This table and all subsequent tables are taken from *Experiences in the
Development of Physical Education, Sports and Recreation as Part of the Formation
and Health of the People. Cuba*. First International Conference of Ministers and
High Representatives in Charge of Physical Education and Sport organised by
UNESCO with the Cooperation of CIEPS, 5–10 April 1976. (Report in
English, French and Spanish.)

Central American and Caribbean Championships were held in Mexico in October 1926 when 136 Mexican, 113 Cuban and twenty Guatemalan sportsmen took part, Cuba staged the second Games in 1930 when eleven countries entered and tennis was introduced for women. There are now sixteen countries eligible, including Jamaica, Trinidad and Tobago, Venezuela, Colombia, Puerto Rico, the Dominican Republic, Mexico and Cuba. These championships are held biannually.

The Pan-American Games, which are modelled more closely on the Olympic Games, began in Buenos Aires in 1951 and are open to all countries in North and South America. Not surprisingly the United States has completely dominated most of the nineteen sports in each of the six Games held, especially the track and field events. In Mexico City, in 1975, Cuba did remarkably well to finish second overall to the USA, ahead of Canada in the unofficial points table, taking twenty-five medals in track and field including seven golds.

The medal table (Table 1) shows the considerable progress made by Cuba in these major championships and the recent Olympic Games and although that progress reflects improvement in all the sports entered, it should be emphasised that Cuban boxers and sprinters have been responsible for a disproportionate degree of this success. Cuban boxers alone have won no less than thirteen medals in the last two Olympic Games and completely dominated the first ever amateur World Championships held in Havana in 1974.

Table 2.   PARTICIPATION IN SPORT IN CUBA

Year	In schools generally	In Cuba	Total
1962	—	104,231	104,231
1963	39,843	129,291	169,134
1964	89,590	309,951	399,541
1965	145,708	586,940	732,648
1966	479,575	778,226	1,257,801
1967	829,950	1,281,224	2,111,174
1968	962,498	1,371,606	2,334,104
1969*	1,062,712	1,177,375	2,240,087
1970	1,233,268	1,094,317	2,327,585
1971	1,086,153	1,214,238	2,300,391
1972	966,821	821,017	1,787,838
1973	1,314,589	1,063,813	2,378,402
1974	1,673,574	1,303,734	2,977,308
1975†	2,136,466	1,367,964	3,504,540

* 1969 onwards, changes in curriculum and exams with higher levels set

† Up to 30 September 1975.

With regard to the national sport baseball, Cuba was again the world champion in 1977, having won this title twice previously in 1971 and 1973. One of the greatest challenges still left open can best be summed up by Fidel Castro:

One day, when the Yankees accept peaceful coexistence with our own country, we shall beat them at baseball too and then the advantages of revolutionary over capitalist sport will be shown![10]

Clearly the Cubans have followed a policy of developing each of their major sports to a good international standard before introducing new sports. At the beginning of 1977, there were thirty-seven officially recognised competitive sports in Cuba with an estimated 3 million participants from a total population of less than 9 million! (see Table 2).

Professional sport is no drain on the amateur ranks as it is in the rest of Central, South and North America but it is clear that many Cuban sportsmen could easily succeed in the professional ranks were it their wish to do so or if the opportunity was readily available. Most would certainly follow the Party line with regard to the rôle of professional sport or rather the lack of its rôle. Castro again, referring to professional sport in pre-1959 Cuba:

Sport . . . what had become of sport? Apart from providing entertainment for the children of rich families in their aristocratic schools and clubs, sport had become a form of business. It had been turned into a piece of merchandise, an object of exploitation . . .[11]

It is interesting to note Teofilo Stevenson's recent reaction to being offered more than US $1 million to fight various American professional heavyweight boxers, albeit in the neutral venue of Jamaica:

What is one million US dollars compared to the love of eight million Cubans?[12]

Philosophy apart, the practical advantages of having no professional sport whatsoever in Cuba mean that there are no promoters or entrepreneurs involved. There is no "gate-money" or prize-money, and where there is no money actually changing hands it is at least easier to maintain rules and standards. Even the soccer Cup Final in Cuba is free to all spectators on a "first come, first served" basis. One curious anomaly arises which acts as a disadvantage when trying to develop international sporting ties with other countries. In *amateur* cycling, for example, there is an annual "round the island" race to which foreign riders are always invited. Most of the Eastern Bloc countries accept but many other European countries write back to ask how much appearance or prize money there will be. Despite reassurances that no one will receive any money at all, invitations are often turned down because they refuse to accept that this is so, or assume that their letters are misinterpreted!

However, there is a fast-growing international exchange of athletes for competition, coaching courses and mere observation, as shown in Table 3.

Table 3.   SPORTING EXCHANGES

	Foreign athletes competing in Cuba			Cuban athletes competing abroad		
Year	Participants	Latin American countries	Other countries	Participants	Latin American countries	Other countries
1961	72	3	4	90	2	6
1962	512	13	22	253	1	4
1963	138	10	21	226	1	12
1964	175	3	22	193	2	13
1965	377	2	22	300	3	20
1966	558	2	52	563	3	16
1967	817	5	42	1100	4	18
1968	480	9	26	503	2	15
1969	746	11	36	773	4	22
1970	525	16	24	746	5	18
1971	1258	11	32	1885	11	28
1972	1156	8	24	1874	12	32
1973	925	13	45	1935	11	31
1974	2074	8	59	2560	14	44
1975*	1619	16	38	3810	13	42

* up to 30 October 1975.

Readers may also be interested to note that Cuba has played host to several world championships since as long ago as 1961. These are shown in Table 4.

Table 4.   WORLD CHAMPIONSHIPS HELD IN CUBA

Year	Sport	Cuban Placing
1961	Baseball (Junior)	2nd
1966	Chess	14th
1967	Underwater Fishing	1st
1969	Fencing	10th
1971	Baseball	1st
1971	Gymnastics	4th
1973	Weight-Lifting	6th
1973	Baseball	1st
1974	Boxing	1st

In the field of foreign technical aid by way of coaches and sports technicians, again many illusions are held in the West. How often does one hear sweeping generalisations like "All their coaches are Russians"? In fact, of the thirty-five national coaches for track and field, for example, only two are Soviet and they are both responsible for the decathlon. Until recently, Leonid Shcherbakov, the Soviet Olympic triple jumper and former world record-holder, was in charge of the excellent squad of Cuban triple jumpers, but he returned to the USSR in 1976. In fairness it must be said that although Alberto Juantorena's Polish coach Zigmunt Zabierzowski returned to Poland following his charge's success in the Montreal Olympic Games, he is sadly missed by Juantorena and it is hoped he will return for a further contract. However, Juantorena still enjoys a close relationship with the Cuban 400-metre specialist coach, Jorge Cumberbatch, with whom he trains daily.

Similarly, the boxers, in particular Teofilo Stevenson, had enjoyed Soviet help in the past, but for the past two or three most successful years all seven national boxing coaches have been Cubans and the national squad is in the very capable hands of Alcides Sagana and Angel Cruz. A comprehensive list of foreign coaches in Cuba since 1961 is given in Table 5.

It is abundantly clear to every visitor to Cuba that there is no lack of aspiration at every level of sport. Cuba has a shortage of teachers, coaches and facilities, but an enormous national effort is being made to meet these deficiencies and no one seems embarrassed at the priority given to sport despite a whole range of social needs competing for resources. One thing is clear: whenever and wherever talent is recognised, it will be nurtured and cared for.

Fabio Ruiz, the "Godfather" of Cuban Sport, suggests

that we are only seeing the beginning of Cuba's sporting revolution. Given another four years and the inspiration of being in Mother Russia at the 1980 Olympics, Cuba will have achieved a great deal more![13]

At the Higher Sports College the professor of physiology, Dr. Jose Yanes, himself a former international wrestler, is even more confident of the future, especially in the traditional areas of boxing and sprinting:

What we are doing merely makes sociological and physiological sense. We have sunshine all the year round, a low protein diet to combat laziness, a high indigenous physical work-rate, low infant mortality, the right ideology and all the natural advantages of Negro sprinters. Forget the exceptions of Hary and the laboratory-trained Borzov. As Cuba becomes the first "developed" country in the Caribbean we shall produce the best sprinters in the world.[14]

Most Cubans are convinced that development in other sports will follow as opportunities are made available. They are certain that they

Table 5. FOREIGN TECHNICAL ASSISTANCE

Year	Sports speci-alists	Country of Origin									
		USSR	Bulg.	Pol.	Czech.	Hung.	GDR	North Korea	Rom.	China	Others
1961	2	—	—	—	2	—	—	—	—	—	—
1962	20	14	1	—	3	—	1	—	—	—	1
1963	12	4	1	1	3	—	1	—	2	—	—
1964	20	13	1	—	1	2	1	—	—	2	—
1965	8	2	1	—	1	—	3	—	—	1	—
1966	33	17	3	1	3	3	5	1	—	—	—
1967	32	18	2	2	2	4	3	1	—	—	—
1968	40	14	4	6	3	8	4	1	—	—	—
1969	44	14	6	6	4	6	3	4	—	—	1
1970	60	22	9	6	6	6	3	6	—	—	2
1971	61	28	9	5	6	8	2	2	—	—	1
1972	65	26	18	4	3	10	2	1	—	—	1
1973	46	17	15	3	3	7	—	1	—	—	—
1974	52	21	14	2	2	7	6	—	—	—	—
1975	54	28	10	1	1	7	7	—	—	—	—

N.B. Many of these visiting coaches and sports specialists came on contract, usually for a three-year period; some renewed those contracts to stay for six years. One former Cuban who has taken American citizenship, Preston Gomez, coach to the famous Los Angeles Dodgers, visits Cuba each year to run coaching clinics on baseball.

will even produce great Negro swimmers and have already gone part of the way by producing one of the four best water polo teams in the world—this despite some Western theories suggesting that the absence of Negro swimmers may be due to physiological rather than socio-economic reasons.

There is no doubt that sport in Cuba has become a vital unifying factor in a country that has only recently known political stablility. The fact that it has had to fight for international recognition has merely strengthened its resolve and makes success all the sweeter now. Perhaps the political dogma and insistent propaganda will become less indigestible to the Western observer as the Revolution matures rather than mellows.

V. *The structure of sport in present-day Cuba*

The basic structure of sport in present-day Cuba follows the fundamental model for other communist-governed states (see over).

Fig. 1 is based on the Soviet model characterised by strong federal

Fig. 1

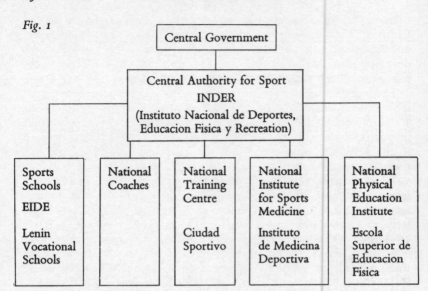

control through the central authority. In Cuba's case this central body is INDER (Instituto Nacional de Deportes Educacion Fisica y Recreacion), which is housed along with the various sports federations at Ciudad Sportivo—the Sports City on the outskirts of Havana. On the same campus are all the training and competition facilities which represent the National Training Centre, the Institute of Sports Medicine and the National Physical Education Institute (ESEF). Adjacent to the Sports City is the site of Cuba's national sports industry. This whole complex represents a most comprehensive range of facilities and organisation within one area. An essential ingredient of this structure is that each State or Province duplicates the national model on a regional basis.

Until recently Cuba had six provinces each with a department of INDER as well as regional training centres and specialist training schools for selected youngsters. The provinces were:

	Population
Pinar del Rio	542,000
La Habana	2,305,000
Mantangas	501,000
Las Villas	1,362,000
Camaguey	813,000
Oriente (subdivided into Holguin and Santiago de Cuba)	2,999,000

However, from January 1977 under the newly-adopted constitution, Cuba is to have fourteen separate provinces plus the Isle of Pines; understandably the structure of the new organisation has still to be developed in terms of facilities, etc. The budget, however, is gradually being expanded to cater for this re-organisation.

The budget allocated by the State to physical education and amateur sport in 1958 (the year preceding the Revolution) is estimated at about a million dollars; there were already about 550 physical education instructors working for the Ministry of Education and funds allocated to the National Institute of Physical Education and Marti Park had risen to $75,000 annually.

These figures do not include the cost of physical education and sport borne by private schools, clubs and companies, nor the cost of professional sport. The former Director of Sport used these funds particularly to promote boxing because it was profitable. Significantly, in 1958 there were about 1,000 unemployed physical education instructors.

In 1975, the revolutionary government allocated more than 50 million pesos to physical education, sport and recreation through INDER, the Ministry of Education (MINED) and other organisations. Examples of INDER budgets are given in Table 6.

Table 6. INDER BUDGET
(in thousands of Pesos)

	1961	1974	1975
Total Expenditure	5295·4	39,892·1	43,576·4
Salaries and wages	1922·7	17,841·9	21,594·1
Other expenses	3372·7	22·050·2	21,982·3
Education (ESEF and EPEF)*		2,396·9	2,654·4
Sports		20,988·3	23,768·7
Recreation		1,305·5	1,358·5
Other activities		15,203·4	15,794·8

N.B. Exchange rate of the Cuban Peso, December 1975:
£1 sterling = 1·675 pesos
US dollar = 82·9 centavos

* ESEF—Provincial Colleges of Physical Education; EPEF—Higher Colleges of Physical Education in Havana

The total number of specialists working in physical education, sport and recreation in 1975 was 7,280, of whom 2,906 worked in INDER and 4,374 were physical education instructors in MINED.

Part of the sports model is the so-called pyramid theory which underlies the competitive sports programme. As far as the Cubans are concerned, in common with the rest of the socialist world, there is no sport without competition. Even the mass participation programme which includes sport for the mentally handicapped and physically disabled is based on the principle that competition is the life-blood of sport. Cubans tend to be both surprised and puzzled by arguments, largely from the West and from educationalists in particular, that play, participation and non-competitive recreation are acceptable in society but that competition somehow breeds anti-social attitudes and is, at least in part, responsible for many undesirable traits in our society.

Clearly the base of the sports pyramid as shown in Fig. 2 is mass participation through school sport, the competitive nub of which is the annual National School Games held each July and covering twenty-two different sports. As Castro has put it,

School Games are reaching a higher standard all the time. We must continue to develop them. We must remember that sport starts when one is very young.[15]

Each level of sports participation then falls into place. One has to appreciate that sport and/or physical education are obligatory both at school, in the armed forces and for the first three years of university life. Progress at sport is closely related to, although not entirely identified with, competition.

Fig. 2

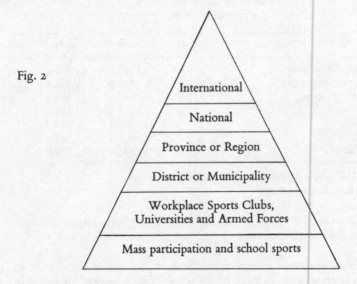

This pyramid structure has to be considered along with linear progress charts, because each group involved in sport follows similar development lines (see following table).

Schools
Workplace Sports Clubs
Armed Forces   } Municipality → Region →
Universities   { Province → National Games
Physically handicapped
Mentally retarded

Furthermore, each sport has the same progress categories for which awards are made, i.e. General Sports Participation or School Sport, on to Junior Sport, Category 2, Category 1, Pre-National selection, National Team.

There is no independent club sport as we know it, nor leagues, and all the various sports (now thirty-seven in Cuba) are integrated rather than fragmented in their organisation and administration. Any athlete in any sport can therefore compare himself or herself with any other athlete in any other sport at any time. This philosophy, which has much to recommend it, argues as follows:

1. The best have to work with the less able at all times.
2. The territory should be more important than the institution or the individual. No prima-donnas!
3. The system works against the concentration of athletic power and in favour of mass participation, albeit in competition.
4. Since everyone participates and sporting progress is linked to educational or work progress, it obviates excessive élitism since the best workers become the best athletes—not the worst workers becoming the best athletes. If you do not advance in studies and in work you cannot participate in sport.
5. No good athletes or teams are lost in the system. Constant motivation and search are encouraged.
6. As soon as teams are selected (on merit rather than whim) there is immediate integration of factory, university, military unit, etc., which is politically and socially desirable.
7. The system avoids recruitment by any one team or unit since no athlete is allowed to move from his home or job without priority being given to his vocational needs.

Two examples may help to demonstrate some of the principles asserted. In order that Teofilo Stevenson may box internationally he must first represent his district or municipality before moving on to the Oriente Provincial Championship, etc. This means that no one is excluded from the lower rungs of the ladder. Where teams progress rather than individuals, not only does the winning team move up, say from Category 2 to Category 1, but in addition a composite team is formed from the best individuals in the district so that no outstanding talent is lost.

Whatever faults the system may have, at least the parameters of the system are known to all and much of the chaos and disharmony caused in the Western world over team or individual selections are avoided. It is also abundantly clear that much of the talent in Cuba has not yet been tapped, especially at district level and in particular with the reorganisation from six to fifteen provinces. The sports programme will not be fully developed for another four or five years. However, one interesting sidelight on the 1976 Montreal Olympic Games was that 60 per cent of the team representing Cuba had been earlier participants as school-children in the Summer Games programme.

Voluntary Sports Councils

It should be emphasised that sport in Cuba, like sport in the West, could not survive without many volunteers who give their time and expertise gratis. Cuba boasts 55,000 sports volunteers to help run its programme and it is constantly recruiting these much respected members of the community, many of whom are either past competitors or simply those who enjoy an identity with sport without being particularly talented. These men and women are members of the Voluntary Sports Councils. They operate in factories, farms and offices, community centres, educational institutions, military units, etc. Their rôle is not merely to organise and administer sports activities and programmes, it is more essentially to promote and popularise sport. They are the people who write the press reports, produce posters and even create their own film and television programmes.

Those countless volunteers without whom British sport could not survive will be interested to know that their Cuban counterparts are much respected and admired for their work by the whole community. It is not the same old thankless task that so often goes on in Britain for years without recognition. Indeed, to be responsible for sports propaganda within large organisations such as the trade unions, the Students Union, the Young Communist League and the Committees for the Defence of the Revolution, is to play a major part in the hierarchy of sport.

Dissimilarities with countries like Britain are particularly marked at the grass roots level. The Voluntary Sports Councils help to organise street and backyard games, play groups, public physical efficiency groups, wherever there is a need or deficiency. They are a driving force of enthusiasts rather than reluctant "volunteers" pressed into service when there is no one else to take on the job. The Cuban volunteers thus become promoters of sport, liaison officers, organisers and talent scouts operating within a national network which covers every community. The grass roots of sports organisation begin with these volunteers.

Table 7. PARTICIPATION IN RECREATIONAL ACTIVITIES

Year	Concha	Shooting	Orient-eering	Roller Hockey	Fishing	Archery	Camping	Games	Total
1963	—	—	—	—	—	—	—	13,993	13,993
1964	—	—	—	—	—	—	—	21,778	21,778
1965	—	—	—	—	—	1,538	—	51,168	52,706
1966	1,441	—	—	—	597	10,067	—	43,053	55,158
1967	4,061	10,300	—	—	879	25,825	—	83,408	124,473
1968	574	6,200	—	4,802	7,859	24,342	—	43,502	87,279
1969	1,840	22,000	—	8,825	10,734	13,316	—	34,641	91,356
1970	2,682	25,250	—	6,473	15,016	8,117	170,227	45,692	273,457
1971	1,599	27,500	—	2,540	48,464	2,836	87,142	4,900,037	5,070,118
1972	7,043	300	—	198	37,551	3,489	73,165	5,256,484	5,378,230
1973	36,339	414	—	6,037	141,959	1,937	92,596	7,489,596	7,769,878
1974	45,295	11,156	2,984	13,862	203,161	1,777	166,186	9,037,699	9,482,120
Oct. 1975	47,649	13,088	7,776	36,477	221,411	4,389	180,108	9,204,202	9,715,100

It certainly would be wrong to assume that everything is available to the consumer in terms of facilities, equipment, organisation, coaches and officials. Much is at a very elementary and unsophisticated level with sports activity encouraged and inspired by parents or youth leaders with improvised equipment. The key to success seems to be a nation-wide publicity campaign for family involvement in sport. It begins with a massive programme of fun and games at street level (Planes de la Calle) which are more akin to the English village fairs or festivals. The sort of activities included are sack races, three-legged races and skipping. Table 7 provides statistics which show the development of the recreational programme and demonstrate not only the success of the programme but the fact that it was the first organised programme for recreation and play activities in the post-revolutionary period. Within the same recreation programme are such activities as archery, fishing, roller hockey, camping, orienteering, shooting and concha (a cross between pelota and squash racquets played under various local rules).

Not only has there been a sharp rise in the number of people taking part, but there has been an equally dramatic rise in the growing number of planned sports activities (see Table 8).

Table 8.   GROWTH IN RANGE OF SPORTS ACTIVITIES

Number of sports pursued:	1958	1963	1968	1975	Increase since 1958
1. Within the school curriculum	2	8	19	22	20
2. Within the public programme	5	22	25	29	24

Another example of mass physical activity is the growing popularity of basic gymnastic and physical-conditioning programmes for women. As well as organised gymnastic classes in clubs and at work-places, there are locally-organised Public Physical Efficiency classes—groups which meet within a housing commune or block of flats. Table 9 indicates how their popularity has grown in recent years.

VI. *Cuban sports industry*

The statistics showing Cuba's success in international sport are all the more impressive when one remembers that in the early post-revolutionary period there was a great dearth of organisation or facilities. At times of revolution chaos and disruption are inevitable, but a further factor seriously hampered Cuba's aspirations. This was the physical

Table 9. THE RANGE AND POPULARITY OF
PRACTICAL PHYSICAL CULTURE

	1972	1973	1974	1975*
1. *Basic Women's Gymnastics*				
Groups	81	875	1,484	2,166
Activities	81	875	1,484	2,043
Participants	4,000	16,417	31,295	50,446
2. *Public Physical Efficiency*				
Groups	107	1,872	1,622	2,428
Activities	107	1,872	1,622	2,393
Participants	2,500	56,213	69,570	80,225
3. *Gymnastics at Work*				
Centres	—	7	68	132
Groups	—	7	92	184
Activities	—	7	107	186
Participants	—	140	2,948	6,778

* Up to October 1975.

N.B. The physical activities referred to are those practised systematically for a minimum of three sessions per week.

blockade of the islands which not only restricted movement but made normal trading and importing impossible.

Since Cuba had little manufacturing capacity and certainly none dealing with sports equipment, even the supply of baseballs of the national game suddenly became an acute problem. So a sports industry had to be created and developed concurrently with a planned programme of sport and recreation. This was by no means easy for a nation of agriculturalists renowned for sugar cane and tobacco.

A further problem was the importation of more sophisticated items of sports equipment which were not easily available from the Eastern Bloc trading partners—such as glass fibre vaulting poles. These and specialist items of gymnastic equipment imported from Japan had to be paid for in hard Western currency; so inevitably supply was very limited.

Nonetheless, the Cubans had to face up to the material needs in terms of equipment if they were going to extend sports and physical education to the masses. A Sports Equipment Factory and various associated branches were then created. Again they leaned heavily on their socialist partners, particularly the Soviet Union, for the engineers and technologists needed to build the factories and install the necessary machinery. The growth of the sports industry is illustrated in Table 10; recent visits have revealed further factories in the process of construction.

Table 10.   SPORTS INDUSTRY

Year	Production Units	Growth in Relation to 1965
1965*	460,015	—
1966	1,494,100	1·62
1967	2,318,630	2·52
1968	3,371,996	3·66
1969	4,097,979	4·45
1970	3,389,374	3·68
1971	5,035,152	5·47
1972	5,552,601	6·04
1973	5,618,720	6·11
1974	7,632,458	8·30
1975†	8,800,000	9·56

* Sports industry was set up in June 1965, therefore the figure refers to second part of year.

† Estimated figure.

One particular recent reward for this hard work and ingenuity has been the acceptance of the Cuban-made baseball as the officially-accepted standard ball for the World Baseball Championships. To add significance to their pleasure at being able to meet the stringent requirements of a world championship sport the Cubans point out that the very first machines used in the manufacturing process were contructed from dismantled pre-revolutionary juke boxes!

All baseball equipment and clothing is now produced by the Cuban sports industry, together with boxing gloves and equipment, football boots, track and field shoes, rowing shells, canoes, sailboats, chess sets, etc. The latest plant, to be opened shortly, has an initial production target of one million balls for various sports each year.

Another interesting facet of the Cuban sports industry is that the Lenin School referred to earlier has a small sports factory where students may elect to work, as an alternative to working in agriculture, for a prescribed ten hours per week.

The whole range of equipment is now widely distributed to schools, colleges and clubs, and is free to all competitors.

In regard to actual facilities, the former private sports clubs were nationalised and made available to the public without charge, along with hotel swimming pools. Even so there are today not nearly enough

facilities to meet demand. May are improvised, others outdated and
in need of repair and refurbishing. It may come as a surprise to many
to learn that Cuba has only one all-weather polyurethane athletics
track—a German Rekortan track laid in 1975. Most of the magnificent
sprinting times and performances by Cuban athletes were made on a
water-bonded shale track at Havana University. During 1977, a second
track of this type is to be opened in Oriente Province and that, along
with many other sports facilities, was in the process of being built during
my December 1976 visit.

An unusual problem which Cuba faces is the actual time taken to
develop many facilities, since they are often built by volunteer workers.
The same workers may well be involved in a communal housing
project which progresses only when labour and materials are available
outside normal working hours.

It is in this particular area of sports facilities that the uninitiated
Western observer would probably be most surprised. Cuba possesses
no lavish community recreation of leisure centres, few swimming
pools outside the pre-revolutionary hotels, no velodrome, ice rink,
regattabahn or indoor diving tank. The facilities for the future are still
on the drawing board, whilst those of the present are largely elementary or even primitive. "Centres of Excellence" in Cuba, to quote
the current fashionable phrase, consist of the coming together of
talented athletes with competent coaches, inspired by lofty aspirations
and surrounded by meticulous medical care.

VII. *The Institute of Sports Medicine* (Instituto de Medicina
    Deportiva)

At the invitation of the Director, Dr. Arnaldo Pallares, I was able to
visit the Institute of Sports Medicine which forms part of the Sports
City complex. Insofar as sports medicine is often neglected in Western
countries, it may be instructive to describe Cuba's medical provisions
for its athletes. Housed in fairly modest buildings, the Institute has a
staff consisting of 142 workers and technicians, forty-two physicians,
seventeen psychologists, six dentists, three biologists, seventeen
physiotherapists, two dieticians, and four statisticians.

The various departments at the Institute are Management and
Administration, Research, Teaching, Medical Assistance given in
conjunction with a local hospital which has a Department of Trau-
matology for surgery, etc., and Physical Development.

Each of the physicians and psychologists has had two years of additional training besides normal medical training. Every sportsman and
woman is examined thoroughly and undertakes a comprehensive
"battery" of tests twice a year. Moreover, each sport has a scientific
brigade responsible for both care and development; these sports are

divided into such groups as endurance sports, explosive sports, ball sports, etc. The physician in charge belongs to the technical committee of the governing body of the sport concerned.

Every national coach has direct contact with the Institute and the Coaching Committee which arranges the annual training programme of each athlete or event group. The Coaching Committees consist of the national coach, a sports physician, a sports psychologist and a member of the technical committee of the governing body who knows the dates and venues of all fixtures.

An interesting point came out in conversation: the psychologists are not used as trained motivators at the major championships; in fact they rarely attend, but they do spend more time training and examining the coaches than the athletes!

Of course, comparisons with sports medical care in one's own country are inevitable and in my case embarrassing, for we in Britain still seek the generous support of a handful of medical and para-medical specialists who give their time freely simply because of their love of a particular sport. Britain has no central institution or central government backing, so there can be few grounds for complaint when things go badly. What is equally embarrassing is the surprise shown by Cubans when they are told of these inadequacies, for they have such a high regard for British traditions for efficiency in sports administration.

VIII. The concept of sport and physical education in Cuban society

(i) Exercise begins at birth

Long before a child's formal education begins in Cuba he or she is encouraged to exercise (and I mean exercise) in addition to play. Physical education begins at birth—or, to be exact, at forty-five days old. Mothers are taught how to massage their babies gently and how to begin exercising their limbs. A number of publications are available to give basic instruction;[16] as the child develops so the exercises, taught as play activities, take a recognisable form such as forward rolls, handstands, cartwheels, headstands, etc. "The Home is the Gymnasium" is the title of one of the instructional pamphlets readily available and published by INDER.

However, it would be wrong to assume that motivation here is geared to the search for precocious talent. Rather the Cuban philosophy is that fun and play, so vital to a child's development, can also include constructive play with "stepping stones" of achievement providing the incentive to instil a real desire for basic health. Castro has a word for it:

All organisations want young people to be vigorous, disciplined and strong in character while remaining happy and cheerful. The whole nation is interested in having children who are equally healthy and happy. Every family, every mother and father, is interested in the health and future of children and in the education they obtain at school. Every Cuban family is therefore interested in physical education and sport for its children.[17]

(ii) *Early selection*

There are certain advantages of early selection which the Soviet Union has long since discovered. Those children with a natural aptitude for, say, gymnastics normally display this aptitude at a very early age and their parents are encouraged to take them to gymnastics or even ballet classes. This also means that formal classes and coaching can begin at a known level of achievement with standards of entry set.

One of the great problems in attempting to develop excellence through coaching in gymnastic classes in Britain, for example, is that the coach is inundated with aspiring young Olga Korbuts who may have no talent whatsoever, yet are not screened and often cannot be denied access to the class. When there is a dearth of facilities and coaches as there is in Cuba, it becomes imperative to be selective if talented children are to realise their ambitions.

Whatever one feels about the somewhat emotive topic of early selection it has to be emphasised that in Cuba sports specialisation is by no means used as an alternative to education. Both education and sport are regarded as pillars of the Revolution and neither must be developed at the expense of the other.

(iii) *Education and sport*

In a country which prides itself on having reduced illiteracy from over 40 per cent to around 4 per cent in a fifteen-year programme, it is difficult to argue that there is any undue emphasis on sport at the expense of education. To be unemployed or to stand outside full-time education is a crime in Cuba. The striking difference for a top-class athlete in Cuba by contrast to some other countries is that it is accepted that the demands of top-class sport are now so great that it may not be possible to excel academically and at sport within the same time span.

This attitude may be illustrated by the example of the double Olympic Champion Alberto Juantorena, who is a student of economics at Havana University. It is accepted that he must train for athletics every day and will be abroad for quite long periods of time, especially for major events like the Olympic Games. His academic programme is therefore adjusted to take four or five years rather than the normal three, and the university seems happy to make the necessary adjustments. He receives a full and generous grant based on his domestic circumstances for the whole time he is at university; the grant is roughly equivalent to what he will earn as an economist when he graduates (in Juantorena's case 320 pesos per month). Therefore, there is no economic urgency to get through university as quickly as possible.

If this is what certain Western observers choose to regard as "professionalism" *vis-à-vis* the Olympic code, then it still must be said that the system has much to commend it over, say, the American scholarship system. In the USA athletes are frequently taken on by colleges for their athletic prowess and never achieve graduation standard or any academic status which is acceptable in the community at large in economic or vocational terms.

A normal working day for Juantorena begins at 8 a.m. at the university where he studies until 1 p.m.; he is then free to train every afternoon. If he does not maintain his university grades his coach and the sports organisation will be informed and he may have to miss certain international trips to make up for lost studies. When questioned about any ultimate clash of interests (i.e. would the Cuban authorities ever ban Juantorena from the Olympics should he fail to show satisfactory progress in his studies?), Cuban officials said that such a decision would be counter-productive. What would happen is that on his return from the Games he would have to concentrate on his studies to make up any lost ground.

The question then arises regarding the less academic. What happens in the case of a factory worker who excels at sport? In such a case, during the time he is absent from work he receives full pay and wherever possible his workmates will work extra hard to meet their missing colleague's quota. Not only do they claim to be proud to do so because they share the joy of his success, but they say that he will do the same for them or their children when he retires from active sport.

It all sounds rather idealistic, but there are so many examples to draw on that it is difficult to refute the evidence. What is more, it is clear that such attitudes in society are inculcated at an early age. They are taught at school and are constantly being reinforced through sports propaganda. To excel at sport in Cuba is regarded in exactly the same way as the whole world regards excellence in art, drama, music or architecture. It is only in some areas of Western society that sport is regarded as a strange bedfellow in such company.

IX. *Physical education and sport at school and college*

(i) *Ordinary and specialist schools*

Following an initiative from Dr. Castro in 1972 in which he suggested that sports training must start earlier despite the lack of trained physical education teachers, the "parents' instruction and progress cards' were introduced for pre-school children. They also began to be used at the 750 day-care centres that have been opened in Cuba for working mothers. These day nurseries are available to all children after their forty-fifth day. Primary education is from six to twelve years of age, and secondary education lasts from 13 to 16 years. Education is based on the principle of combining study with manual work at the secondary level. Adult education centres give basic education to over 400,000 people each year; the current development programme shows that more than 100 new schools are being opened annually.

Physical education and sport as a subject is compulsory in all schools and colleges and in all universities until the third full year. Chess is included in the sports programme and awards in all sports are given for progress rather than for excellence. In all schools, sport is the focal point of all physical education programmes and competition is regarded as the basis of sport. I had no opportunity to visit primary schools but I understand that physical education occupies them for an hour each day.

In the secondary schools, the compulsory sports are track and field, gymnastics, basketball, volleyball and baseball for boys, with modern gymnastics on a competitive basis as an alternative sport for girls. Swimming is also compulsory where facilities exist, but very few schools have their own pools. The obligatory sports were carefully chosen not just to uphold long-standing traditions in Cuban sport, but because they are regarded as being ideal for children's physiological development. As a basic foundation for all other sport and indeed for life, these sports are said to produce a good balance of strength, speed, endurance, agility, power and co-ordination.

It is interesting to note that in many discussions with leading Cuban physical educationalists, I met puzzlement that we in Britain should regard ourselves as capable of teaching so many different sports and recreational activities within the school curriculum rather than in teaching them in specialist clubs outside school. It was difficult to answer the criticism that surely many of our children became "dabblers" at many things and rarely got effective exercise unless they trained systematically for a sport.

Apart from the five basic sports, there has been a marked and steady increase in the number of other sports which are now practised by school-children. Much of this is made possible by the specialist sports schools. Thus, the Summer School Sports Programme (Junior Olympics) has developed from two sports in 1958 to the present twenty-two, and provides first-class competition for all age groups in each of the six provinces. Since there are now to be fifteen separate provinces in Cuba this will change the structure of the Summer Games programme and create more opportunities for selective competition. In the past, each of the six regions had specialist residential schools where talented young-sters attend the EIDE sports schools. Applications for scholarships are made on behalf of the children by teachers or parents. These sports schools normally cater for several sports but there are separate schools for swimming, diving and synchronised swimming. Since all children's physical abilities are tested and measured every three months, selection becomes relatively easy.

(ii) The Isles of Pines ("Isle of Youth")

In 1969 the Isle of Pines, some 2,200 square kilometres in size and situated to the south of Cuba (and said to be the original Treasure Island) was handed over to the youth of Cuba as the land of the future. Now designated the Isle of Youth it is the home of massive citrus groves and some twenty-eight residential secondary schools.

Each boarding or semi-boarding coeducational school caters for between 500 and 600 children and is generally purpose-built in the heart of the citrus groves to enable schoolchildren to work in the production or the canning of the fruit. Most of the students are ferried from Havana on Sunday evenings, returning to their homes on Friday evenings.

Many of the schools specialise in various sports, but there are also language schools as well as art and technical institutions. A school that I visited called the "14th of July" (in commemoration of the date on which it was opened by Fidel Castro in 1973) had a nearby lake for canoe and rowing training, but the 400-metre athletics track was in a fairly dilapidated state. I confess to having felt somewhat relieved to find that the three obligatory hours of work by children each day on the orange groves included a fair amount of skylarking and work-dodging. (It confirmed that children are still children whatever the regime!) In addition to the obligatory manual work, each child has five hours of daily schooling which includes up to two hours of sport. At this school and the others I visited there was every sign that the children enjoyed their environment enormously and I could not help thinking it provided a well-balanced education for life.

(iii) The Lenin School

I shall always wonder whether my comparison of the highly élitist Lenin School just outside Havana to English Public Schools prevented me from ever getting inside, like so many other tourists visiting Cuba. Despite advance permission being given, on three occasions when we came to film this famous school we were turned away firmly but politely on what appeared to be the flimsiest of excuses. Since we had been asked to submit the film profile in writing and I had made what

I thought to be an obvious but honest comparison, I can only wonder and regret not having seen the school in detail.

It is a secondary school (7th–13th grades) for 4,500 academically brilliant pupils. Prior to entrance, school work is assessed from course work and examinations over the previous three years. In 1976, entry was limited to those who had achieved 97 per cent in their assessment.

Besides its high academic standards, the school is Cuba's *pièce de résistance* in terms of sports, with international-standard facilities for twenty-two sports, including a 50-metre pool with separate diving pool and 10-metre platform, 400-metre track, gymnasia, tennis, basketball and volleyball courts, weight training rooms, baseball diamonds, etc.

A further interesting feature of the Lenin School is that, in addition to the many acres of farmland worked by the pupils, it has its own factory for the manufacture of sports equipment. The school's proud boast was that its pupils had, by 1976, produced goods to the total value of one million pesos.

Even selection on the basis of academic ability, rather than wealth, still seems to me to encourage élitism; the school is clearly Cuba's show-place.

(iv) *The Summer Games or Junior Olympic Programme*

The competitive focal point of all sports in Cuban schools is the Summer Games which take place in July most years, but the date varies with the state of the sugar harvest. This is the culmination of a massive programme of local, district and regional championships and evidently provides the basis for much of Cuba's international sporting success. As stated earlier, more than 60 per cent of Cuba's Montreal squad had previously taken part in the Junior Olympic Programme, which was established in 1963 and has since been expanded to include the following twenty sports:

Chess	Weightlifting
Athletics	Tennis
Soccer	Table Tennis
Basketball	Modern Gymnastics
Gymnastics	Synchronised Swimming
Swimming	Diving
Volleyball	Water Polo
Cycling	Fencing
Judo	Pistol Shooting
Baseball	Wrestling

Although competitions exist for each year within the secondary-school age groups, the overall championships are decided on the results of two broad categories: juniors under thirteen, and seniors under sixteen. In some sports, like swimming and gymnastics, the lowest age groups are 9–10 years (see Table 11).

Table 11. PARTICIPANTS IN SCHOOL AND JUNIOR GAMES AT NATIONAL LEVEL

| | Seniors (13–16) | | Juniors (under 13) | |
Course	Participants	Sports in Programme	Participants	Sports in Programme
1962–3	3,478	8	—	—
1963–4	2,491	8	—	—
1964–5	3,200	8	—	—
1965–6	3,355	10	—	—
1966–7	4,398	16	—	—
1967–8	4,998	19	—	—
1968–9	4,978	19	—	—
1969–70	4,978	19	—	—
1970–1	4,990	19	1,109	8
1971–2	4,946	19	1,234	16
1972–3	4,150	19	1,198	14
1973–4	4,156	20	1,586	17
1974–5	4,626	22	1,818	17

N.B. The same sports and events have not been programmed in all the Games.

Progress for individuals and teams follows well-defined lines. From their own school championships, successful athletes move up to district, area and regional championships. From the Junior Olympic programme successful juniors may join the regional teams which then integrate with teams representing various industries, the military and students, and then go on to Category 2, Category 1, and finally to the national squads.

All inter-school games play "A" and "B" sides on the same day to enable many of the less able to compete; when one team progresses to the next stage a composite team is made up of the best individuals from all the losing teams so that no outstanding individual is lost.

(v) The Higher Institute of Physical Education

The Escuola Superior de Educacion Fisica was opened as a higher institute of physical education in 1972. Prior to that it was the Havana Regional College of Education which specialised in physical education in a similar way to colleges in the other regions. It is situated in the Sports City (Ciudad Sportivo) on the outskirts of Havana in the same complex as INDER, the Institute of Sports Medicine and the Sports Industry. Both ordinary students and practising first division sportsmen and women are accepted for four years training in three separate discipline areas:

1. Sports—to train as coaches and instructors
2. Physical Education—to train as specialist teachers
3. Recreations—to train as youth leaders and recreationalists.

All students have a basic education in the three disciplines and must be capable of teaching the fundamentals of each discipline. In addition they must specialise in one sport and take a second sport as a subsidiary subject. Many of the students have already spent four years in a regional college of physical education and are now studying for the equivalent of a Master's degree. This means, in fact, that future Cuban national coaches in many sports will have had eight years of specialist higher education!

Practising teachers who want to return to college to update or further their training can do so on a full-time or part-time basis, while retaining a full teacher's salary (approximately 225 pesos per month). On reaching higher degree status, their salaries are increased to just over 300 pesos per month.

The higher sports institute has an exchange arrangement with other socialist countries as well as with other Latin American states. It even has one girl student from the United States. The college authorities are seeking a far wider international exchange, although it has to be remembered that the college has only existed in its present state for five years. As the college evolves it hopes to achieve university status for its doctoral degrees, but at the moment it admits that research is difficult owing to lack of information in the various disciplines. Clearly, the institute will have a significant rôle to play in the future development of sport and physical education at all levels. Among Castro's many utterances on the rôle of sport in education, the following sums up the aims most pithily:

One day we shall have thousands of young people studying physical education, excellent sports facilities in all schools, and inter-schools competitions as a means of selection. However, there is more to it than selection, for sport should be pursued not just to win competitions. Competitions are important, medals are important; but there is something more important—sport as a cultural and recreational activity for the people. Of course, if everybody practises a sport, if all children pursue a sport, we shall have champions.[18]

For someone like myself whose whole life has practically been concerned with physical education and sport, a visit to Cuba is an invigorating and englightening experience. To the cynics who might suggest that I only saw what they wanted me to see, I would only say that I have visited some fifty countries and that such a wealth of experience makes deception difficult. To those who may feel that I have sold my soul to the communist ideology of sport, I can only maintain that to me sport in Britain still has many attractions and advantages over the rest of the world. But if I were living in the Third World and seeking an identity through sport, seeking to democratise sport for a modernising society, there are many principles and aspects of Cuban sport that I would readily adopt.

NOTES

1. D. Anthony, "Comparative Physical Education", *Physical Education*, LVIII, November 1966, pp. 70–3; and unpublished doctoral thesis "Comparative Physical Education", University of Leicester.
2. Maxwell L. Howell, "Sources for Comparative Physical Education and Sport", Edmonton, Alberta; University of Alberta (*c.* 1967).
Bruce L. Bennett, Maxwell L. Howell, and U. Simri, *Comparative Physical Education and Sport*, Lea and Febiger, Philadelphia, 1975.
3. Information in this section is taken mainly from the following sources: *Encyclopaedia Britannica*, Vol. 5; *Europa Year Book*, 1976, Vol. II; *Statesman Yearbook*, 1976–7.
4. "Basketball Diplomacy", *Sunday Times*, 10 April, 1977.
5. *Fidel, Sobre el deporte*, edited by Sonia Castanes, Havana, 1975, para. 368 (speech made in 1974).
6. *El Deporto*, Ano 9, No. 3, 1976.
7. *Fidel*, op. cit., para. 40 [1960].
8. Ibid, para. 293 [1971].
9. Ibid, para. 362 [1974].
10. Ibid, para. 91 [1962].
11. Ibid., para. 67 [1961].
12. Maule, Tex, *Sports Illustrated*, March 1974.
13. Personal communication.
14. Personal communication.
15. *Fidel*, op. cit., para. 316 [1971].
16. For example, *Matro Gimnasia*, pamphlet issued by INDER to parents; *Mama, Papa, Hagan Ejercicios Conmigo*, by Jana Berdychova (INDER).
17. *Fidel*, op. cit., para. 76 [1961].
18. Ibid, para. 368 [1974].

INDEX